A careless word may kindle strife;
a cruel word may wreck a life;
a bitter word may hate instill;
a brutal word may even kill;
a gracious word may smooth the way;
a joyous word may light the way;
a timely word may lessen stress;
a loving word may heal and bless.
—*author unknown*

*T*hose who use words of disparagement rather than words of encouragement do so thinking that, by lowering the other person, they are raising themselves. Actually, the opposite is true. *What we put out, we get back.*

Life Without Limits brings you the tools you need to improve your own luck, circumstances, and happiness, while bringing greater joy and prosperity into the lives of those around you.

Discover the culprit that acts to block your joy . . . learn how to dramatically improve your luck . . . use body language to attract others . . . talk yourself into wealth . . . solve any problem no matter where you are . . . and eliminate the fears and phobias that hold you back. The journey to success begins with a single thought. Transform your thinking and unveil the limitless life that awaits you.

~

About the Author

Robert B. Stone, Ph.D., is the author and co-author of over 86 published books, several with sales of over a million copies, as well as scores of magazine articles, most recently one in *Cosmopolitan*. He has lectured worldwide on human potential and was a past instructor at the University of Hawaii on activating the powers of the mind. A MENSA member, he has a degree from the Massachusetts Institute of Technology and was elected to the New York Academy of Science. A Silva Method lecturer for 20 years and Ambassador-at-Large for the Silva Method for 10 years, he introduced the Silva Method in Japan, New Zealand, India, the Soviet Union, and Thailand. Married to his wife Lola for 45 years, he lives in Thailand and continues to help bring out the guru in others.

To Write to the Author

If you wish to contact the author or would like more information about this book, please write to the author in care of Llewellyn Worldwide and we will forward your request. Both the author and publisher appreciate hearing from you and learning of your enjoyment of this book and how it has helped you. Llewellyn Worldwide cannot guarantee that every letter written to the author can be answered, but all will be forwarded. Please write to:

Robert B. Stone, Ph.D.
℅ Llewellyn Worldwide
P.O. Box 64383, Dept. K698-X
St. Paul, MN 55164-0383, U.S.A.

Please enclose a self-addressed stamped envelope for reply, or $1.00 to cover costs. If outside U.S.A., enclose international postal reply coupon.

ROBERT B. STONE, PH.D.

Life
Without
LIMITS

10 Easy Steps to
Success & Happiness

1998
Llewellyn Publications
St. Paul, Minnesota 55164-0383, U.S.A.

FIRST EDITION
First Printing, 1998

Book design by Rebecca Zins
Cover art by Digital Stock Photography
Cover design by Anne Marie Garrison
Edited by Pam Keesey and Rebecca Zins

Library of Congress Cataloging-in-Publication Data
Stone, Robert B.
    Life without limits: 10 easy steps to success & happiness /
Robert B. Stone.—1st ed.
            p.   cm.
    Includes bibliographical references and index.
    ISBN 1-56718-698-X (pbk.)
    1. Conduct of life.   2. Quality of life.
    3. Success—Psychological aspects.   4. Happiness.
    I. Title.
    BF637.C5S716   1998
    158—dc21   98-28150
                                                          CIP

Printed in the U.S.A.

Llewellyn Publications
A Division of Llewellyn Worldwide, Ltd.
P.O. Box 64383, Dept. 698-X
St. Paul, MN 55164-0383, U.S.A.

Contents

The Superior Person Encourages People at Their Work . . .
How You Can Help Yourself by Boosting Others . . . OK,
Good Begets Good, but How Does It Work? . . . How Good
Begets Good in the Business World . . . Why Good Is
Contagious in Any Activity . . . How to Make a Dramatic
Improvement in Your Own Luck, Circumstances, and
Happiness . . . Two Steps to Change the Polarity of Your
Thinking . . . How to Relax Deeply to Turn On Your
Mental Computer . . . How to Program Your Mental
Computer . . . Some Positive Affirmations that
Transform Your Thinking

2: Step Off the Treadmill of Limited Money and Limited Love Now . . . 23
from Konedda, Druid priest and counselor

The Druids, the Oak Tree, and You . . . How to Profit from a Druid Secret . . . Two Exercises that Begin to Open the Door . . . Why the Poor Get Poorer and the Rich Get Richer . . . Poor or Rich—the Choice Is Yours . . . A Simple Procedure to Cause a Shift in Consciousness from Poverty to Plenty . . . A Similarity Between Nightdreaming and Daydreaming . . . The Amazing Ability You Acquire at the Alpha Brain Frequency . . . There Are No Limits to the Power of Your Mind to Bring Wealth and Love . . . The Act of Reuniting with Your Higher Self . . . This One Minute Is Priceless to You . . . How to Make the Flame Burn Brighter . . . How to Send Out a Call for More Love and Wealth

3: The Amazing Power of Positive Imaging . . . 45
from Panopoulos, Greek naturalist

Seeing with the Mind Yields Insight . . . Objective and Subjective Uses of the Inner World . . . Write Your Own Ticket While in the Creative State . . . To Think Positively Is to Be Part of the Solution, Not Part of the Problem . . . One Daydream that Provides You with a Winning Ticket . . . The Problems of the World that Need Your Help . . . How to Help Solve Any Problem No Matter Where It Is . . . How to Keep in Touch with Your Creativity . . . Adopting a Special Way to Be Closer to the Creator . . . Positive or Negative Thinking—A Continuous Effort . . . How to Get Help from Nature in Improving Your Lot in Life . . . Mental Housecleaning as a Prerequisite to Positive Thinking

9: Acquiring an Invisible Means of Support . . . 189
from Swami Amara of India

West versus East—Material versus Spiritual . . . Which
Came First, the Spiritual or Material Realms? . . . Where the
Spiritual Cause of the Material Effect Lies . . . The Right Steps
May Not Be the Same for Everybody . . . How to Speak the
Creator's Language . . . The Whole Is Greater than the Sum
of Its Parts . . . The True Meaning of Greatness . . . Reaching
Your Goal Even When the Going Gets Tough . . . The Wheel
of Fortune and How to Make It Spin for You . . . Everyday
Factors that Facilitate Help from the Other Side . . . How to
Win an Argument with a Materially Minded Person

10: Ways to Magnify Your Magic . . . 213
summarized by Dr. Robert B. Stone

How to Make the Most of Your Time on This
Planet . . . The Way Life Is on Earth . . . How One Mind
Can Help More than One Life . . . Where Consciousness
Goes, A Real Energy Goes . . . Reinforcing Your Connection
to the Other Side . . . Time Is Different on the Other Side
(If It Exists at All) . . . The Creator and You—An Unbeatable
Team . . . Benefits that Are Now Attainable by You . . .
How Scientists Are Slowly Bending in God's Direction . . .
You Have Made a Quantum Leap Ahead of Scientists . . .
The Unconscious Exposed for What It Really Is . . .
The Oneness of the Universe Has You at Its Center

Bibliography . . . 235

&xercises

$\mathcal{P}$reface

I have participated in 86 self-help or inspirational books either as the sole author or co-author. But I have made one monumental mistake. Before I explain that mistake, let it be stated unequivocally here and now that in this book the mistake is corrected.

To explain the mistake, here is how I usually proceed with a book. I carefully select sources of material that I believe will be helpful—books, pamphlets, news clippings, and periodicals. I stack these within reach of where I write, which happens to be just to my left. I am not unaware that a person's left side is the receiving side. And I begin.

Several months later, when the manuscript has been completed, that stack of resource material has been untouched. All of the information has come to me directly or through other means. Now, about my mistake:

I have conceived myself to be the author. Whereas the information has been divinely supplied through the Creator's infinite channels, I have turned my back on these channels and never once acknowledged their contributions.

This error is now corrected. British biologist Rupert Sheldrake, who conceived the existence of a morphogenetic field of intelligence to which we are all connected (which Carl Jung called the collective unconscious), has supplied the key.

Controlled daydreaming connects us to this larger intelligence. And I, with the assistance of my wife Lola, have meditated on the particular past or present sources of wisdom who have helped me with this manual for successful living. This has been done chapter by chapter. By relaxing and daydreaming about who deserves my thanks for each chapter, the particular sage has come to mind.

These sources have been listed at the start of each chapter and thanked in the Acknowledgments, and now I may breathe a sigh of relief.

That is how this has become a manual for successful living. It details the steps to take, sometimes surprising and even quite contrary to humanity's generally accepted ways, toward a life without limits.

~

Acknowledgments

I thank the nine sages who were my unseen sources.

Help for this work came largely from my experience with 86 other published books that I authored or co-authored, but getting down to a finer focus, I merit its materialization in its present form to Joanne Spletter, typist extraordinaire; Rebecca Zins and Pam Keesey, editors beyond compare; and Lola, wife in its fullest scope.

~

1

A Different World Awaits for You to Push the Right Button

~from Lo Fu, Chinese poet and philosopher

Philosopher Henry Thoreau wrote, "Most men lead lives of quiet desperation." But that was about one hundred years ago. Times have changed. They have gotten worse.

Today, make that "All men and women lead lives of quiet desperation."

Why is everybody so persistently desperate? They have a number of reasons: job, health, children, drugs, security, crime, politics, war, taxes, strangers, education, violence, environment, traffic, noise, prices, neighbors. Surely you can add a few more.

What can you do about it?

This book answers that question. The answer is provided in ten installments, one to each chapter. These installments are simple changes to make in the way you are doing things, as simple as pushing a button and having a door open for you.

I am not your doorman. I am assisted by nine wise men and women who lived in the last thousand years, each leaving behind a valuable legacy for a joyful, desperation-free life—a legacy that has either remained hidden, forgotten, or ignored all these years. One of these seers is the hidden source for each chapter and is introduced in the opening paragraphs.

One reason these legacies have remained hidden is that they have been buried in other cultures' literature, which is both voluminous and distant.

One example is the I Ching, the Chinese Book of Changes, a book so chock full of wisdom that it became the equivalent of a Bible to generations of Chinese rulers.

Hiding in the I Ching is one of the most powerful of all life-changing forces:

The Superior Person Encourages People at Their Work

This can be shortened to: The superior person encourages people. It can also be clarified when worded this way: A person who encourages people becomes superior.

In other words, if you put people up, you are putting yourself up.

Wow! Does that mean the supervisor under whom you used to work, who criticized everybody left and right, was on the wrong track? Yes, he was on the wrong track. He will receive his "come-uppance" in the form of a "come-downance," if he hasn't already.

The person who prefers to use a word of disparagement rather than a word of encouragement does so thinking that, by lowering the other person, he is raising himself.

The opposite is true. We will discuss why in a moment.

Lo Fu was a Chinese poet and philosopher who lived in the mid-eighth century. She was a devotee of the I Ching and used it liberally in her work. She lived in Hangchow, near the famous Wu Lake District, at a time when China was enjoying the height of the Tang Dynasty, one of the greatest periods in its history.

Despite her contemplative life, Lo Fu attracted many disciples to whom she taught reverence for life and techniques for attaining inner tranquility. She believed in raising people's self-esteem, a step that always changed their lives for the better.

The writers of the I Ching knew millennia ago what we are just beginning to understand today: The importance of high self-esteem to a person's success.

Remember the old story of how the king criticized his advisor, his advisor cursed the jester, the jester bawled out the maid, the maid scolded the footman, and the footman kicked the dog?

Put-downs are catching. So are put-ups. Rewrite that old story as a chain of put-ups and it might sound something like this: A parent encourages the child, the child thanks the teacher, the teacher positively radiates to the class, the class turns in record grades, and when the class members graduate, they recommend the school.

What does all this have to do with you? Plenty.

How You Can Help Yourself
by Boosting Others

Remember hearing this rhyme years ago?

> A careless word may kindle strife;
> a cruel word may wreck a life;
> a bitter word may hate instill;
> a brutal word may even kill;
> a gracious word may smooth the way;
> a joyous word may light the way;
> a timely word may lessen stress;
> a loving word may heal and bless.

> —*author unknown*

Strife in whom? Wreck whose life? Instill hate where? Kill whom? Smooth and light whose way? Lessen stress in whom? Heal and bless whom?

You, you, you.

The words that you choose to levy on others come back to roost on you. Perhaps they intuitively understood this millennia ago, in the days of the I Ching, but today we have a scientific explanation.

It is a simple energy interchange. What we put out, we get back. If our life expresses negativity in word or deed, Life with a capital "L" replaces it with its equal.

⌒Philip was sure he was somebody special when he was a teenager. It so happens he was right, but nobody else knew it. Frustrated, he told everybody how good he was by criticizing everybody and telling them how wrong *they* were. It did not work. They thought less and less of him. One day, he heard his father speak highly of him to a neighbor. The neighbor hired Philip part-time. It helped ease his frustration. It also shone a light on what he was doing. He decided to change polarity and boost himself—not by criticizing others, but by boosting them. Suddenly, he was on top of the world in his peers' estimation. Today he is a respected scientist.

There is a power at work throughout the universe, and more pertinently in this world called Earth, which assists each living thing not only to survive but to rise to a higher life form. This power is commonly known by a three-letter word, but we will use the word "Creator" instead. The word "God" has been overused to the point where its impact has been lost.

The reason the Creator is assisting us to rise to a higher state of being is because creation is incomplete. It is still in process. And we are all involved in that ongoing process. We are like co-creators, busy making this a better world to live in. Except . . . not involved in this upgrading process and, therefore, not being upgraded themselves, are the downgraders. If you were the Creator, would you help those who are destroyers rather than creators? Hardly.

You can help yourself wholly by being a creator rather than a destroyer. This means you can enjoy more life energy, enabling you to radiate a higher level of wellness, function more skillfully, demonstrate dependable intuition, and solve more difficult problems.

A boy falls off a bicycle. You help to dust him off, get back on, and continue his ride confidently. A girl is timidly wearing a new dress; you compliment her, telling her how princess-like she looks. Your landlord stops by for the rent. You say how well things have been going in the house, even if you have to close your eyes to a few minor problems.

There are so many ways to help people. It is not all ushering a blind old lady across the street. Nor is it just a smile and a pat on the back.

> ⁓Georgene paid part of the college tuition of a less fortunate neighbor's daughter. She asked nothing in return. But whether she asked or not, the universe insisted that good deserves good. Her own professional career prospered beyond her greatest expectations.

So it is that the universe must, according to its own laws, pay you back for freely given favors. And the universe pays higher than minimum wage.

OK, Good Begets Good, but How Does It Work?

To understand how your doing good brings good to you, it is best to start where you are—in your body. Later, we will see how this microscopic view is extrapolated from a macroscopic view of the universe.

It is probably not news to you that the mind runs the body. Although a relative newcomer to the health picture, this fact has received so much exposure in the media in recent years[1] that younger doctors are beginning to accept the concept and several prestigious medical schools, i.e., Harvard Medical School, are beginning to teach it.

---

1. Stone, Robert B. *Mind/Body Communication*. Niles, Ill: Nightingale-Conant, 1993.

If the mind runs the body, then a habitually positive mind should result in a healthier body and a habitually negative mind should produce an ailing body. Let's look at the record to see if this pans out.

Brain/Mind, a monthly newsletter encapsulating scientific research in this area, reports in its November 1995 issue that the Institute of Heart Math has found that feelings of anger produce a negative effect on the body, while feelings of appreciation cause a positive effect.

In the former situation, namely anger, the sympathetic branch of the autonomic nervous system was activated. This caused the heart rate to accelerate and the arteries to constrict, symptoms also associated with heart disease and death.

On the other hand, feelings of appreciation for another person were found to affect the parasympathetic branch of the autonomic nervous system. This branch is considered protective of the body's health. Electromagnetic heart patterns became more coherent—a characteristic of wellness—and levels of immunoglobin-A were higher. Immunoglobin-A is the body's first line of defense against infection and disease.

Rollin McCraty, who headed the research team for Heart Math, called this the first real proof that "love and appreciation are healthier than anger."

Of course, other mind/body relationships underline this same precept: That positive feelings promote positive physical results and that negative feelings can seriously erode health.

Some examples are in your manner of speech. If you habitually use negative statements referring to parts of the body, they can eventually come true and manifest as illness.

Perhaps you say, "He gives me a pain in the neck." If you awaken in the morning with a stiff or sore neck, think back to who "gave" it to you.

Perhaps you say, "She makes me sick." Say it frequently enough and she will do exactly that.

Do you occasionally say, "That breaks my heart"? Better stop. Or, "I can't stand him (or her)"? You're not doing your legs any good.

What cyberphysiology—the mind/body connection—entails is your willingness to feel genuine love for your body. You then express that love to whatever part of your body is not functioning perfectly. You do this by relaxing and imaging the internal organ or system. You "see" it responding to your mental pictures of perfect functioning. You express a sincere love and thank it for its good work.

What would happen if, instead, you berated that organ for its problems? Do this often enough and you would very likely be signing your death knell.

Good begets good. That's how it works inside you. Now, how does it work on Main Street?

How Good Begets Good in the Business World

We've established that good is contagious. So is bad. Take your pick. The choice is available to us every minute of every day, whether we are at home or away, at work or at play.

The business world is perhaps the most difficult environment in which to make that choice. The reason is that the good path is more likely to be less profitable than the bad, at least from an immediate point of view.

Attendance is lagging in your theater. You are losing money. Raise the price of tickets, you say. That sounds like the solution. So you do. And you make more money, but now some people find the movies too expensive. They stay home and watch television. Your gross take goes down instead of up. Does that mean next time you will know better? Don't bet on it.

You are in the food business. Lower quality costs less and you can make more. Your customers won't know the difference. So you supply lower quality. Your net profit jumps. But soon your customers are going across the street, where the quality is higher. At the end of the year, your lower volume of sales puts you in the red, while across the street there is a grocer who is all smiles.

Management and labor are constantly in a state of confrontation in the United States. Each wants a bigger portion of the pie. As a result, the consumer pays a bigger bill for products and services. Inflation becomes rampant, and everybody loses.

What would happen if both management and labor lived by the principle of not who is right, but what is right? How does one define "what is right"? Usually what is right means that which makes their world a better world to live in.

Now we are getting somewhere. Think about it. Is this the best of all possible worlds? Far from it. That means creation is nowhere near completion. Perhaps that is why the Creator has put us here—to help with the completion of creation.

Why Good Is Contagious
in Any Activity

Anyone who thinks negatively is an ally of destruction rather than a friend of creation.

We cannot all be like that little boy who refused to leave the manure-filled barn. When asked why he kept digging in it, he replied, "With all this manure here, there must be a pony somewhere."

Still, it's easy to be positive. Anyone who thinks positively is an ally of creation. Such a person is a co-creator with the Creator. Help make this a better world to live in and you share the abundance that is already here.

You not only find that you are in a flow of money quite adequate to pay bills and buy what you'd like, but you are rich in the other aspects of abundance so essential to true prosperity: loving friends, romance, joy, and inner peace.

When you think positively, your actions reflect those positive thoughts. It is impossible to feel optimistic, supportive, constructive, and appreciative without actually being helpful, creative, loving, and contributory.

If you do something in your work that you are not really required to do, but it helps solve a problem, should you put in a charge for overtime?

If a visitor spots a book on a shelf in your living room, one you have already read, which your visitor is intrigued with, and which you decide to part with, do you charge your visitor a fair used-book price?

Your waiter is exemplary. He explains the menu, replaces an improperly prepared dish, advises you on desserts, and looks in on you to see if all is well. Do you leave him a generous tip?

There is a good reason not to charge for overtime; the same good reason not to charge for the book; and a good reason in favor of a higher than usual tip. That good reason is not to ingratiate yourself with your boss or with the visitor or with the waiter. It is to ingratiate yourself with the Creator.

You won't find why in any encyclopedia, book of knowledge, or compendium of wisdom. But it is carved in the stone of human experience: The Creator does not allow good to go unrewarded, and the rewards far exceed minimum wage.

Khahil Gibran, author of *The Prophet*, has said, in effect, Don't invite rich people to your house for dinner. They will repay you by inviting you to their house for dinner. Invite poor people to your house for dinner. They cannot pay you back, so the universe must pay you back.

The universe is sure to pay you back. It is a law as immutable as the law of gravity.

This does not mean that businesses should give away their products or services. They would soon have to close their doors. That would be destructive, not creative. It would make this a lesser world to live in.

What it behooves you to give away are your favors and helpful acts both outside and inside of your livelihood. Sometimes it is better to charge for something that has been free. For instance . . .

〜The chief librarian of a state-run Western university was faced with severe budget cuts because of a state revenue shortfall that affected all branches of the government, including this university. The librarian had been with the university for over ten years and had built up the library to where it was one of the most complete in the country.

Now he was faced with practically no new acquisitions, a reduction in periodicals, and shorter hours. Other department heads, faced with similar cuts, merely threw up their hands in surrender and said, "So be it." Not this librarian.

"I am a problem-solver, not a problem victim," he reminded himself and others. He made the plight of the library known and instituted a thirty dollar annual fee for the use of the library. Money poured in. Even people who never used the library paid their thirty dollar membership fee to support the library's excellent status. As a result, that university still has one of the best libraries in the country despite the budget cuts, thanks to a positive thinking problem-solver.

How to Make a Dramatic Improvement in Your Own Luck, Circumstances, and Happiness

We live in an energy field. It fills all space. Here is some good news and some bad news about this field of energy. First the good news: scientists have discovered God. Now the bad news: they won't admit it. Actually, this energy is the source of all life and in every atom of matter.

It does not matter what scientists call this field. What is important is that it functions as a field of intelligence. It is the closest we can come to conceiving the Creator. It is this intelligence that keeps the universe running.

It is this intelligence that also keeps us running. Besides keeping us running, it joins with our own personal intelligence to bring us instinct, ideas, intuition, and inspiration.

Those of us who are more in tune with a universal outlook attract this field of intelligence more than do those who think more limitedly. Those of us who are close to nature in our ways are bound to have this universal outlook, which really amounts to an appreciation of living things. Those of us who realize that the material world we live in is not the source of existence, but rather such source is in the creative realm and, therefore, a spiritual source, are in line for amazing joy in life.

I was traveling in Greece some years ago and visited some ancient ruins that were still being excavated. One structure, for which few attachments were yet uncovered, was identified as a type of clinic. There, patients were given what the healers of that day administered. Their healing work did not stop at night. There were pipes going down from the healers' headquarters to each bed. These pipes were used for communication. At night the healers sent positive suggestions to the sleeping patients. One may postulate that these suggestions were simple statements along the lines of "You are getting better every day" or "The medicine is working and getting rid of your illness."

People can reach their own body-controlling minds on their own, and do so while awake. It is the key to acquiring all of the attitudes mentioned so far in this chapter.

Back in the 1950s, Dr. Hornell Hart, professor of sociology at Duke University, introduced what he called "auto-conditioning." It was a way of changing attitudes from negative to positive. It consisted of two steps:

1. Relaxing the body and mind.
2. Instructing yourself to have positive attitudes and constructive behavior.

Since then, a number of approaches to the same goals have been popularized. Examples are hypnotism and self-hypnotism. They took a hint from Emil Coué, a French lecturer, who had thousands of people on two continents looking in a mirror and repeating over and over, "Every day, in every way, I am getting better and better."

Coué supplied the impetus to the use of suggestion. The ultimate use of suggestion arrived about twenty-five years ago in the form of a four-day training course called the Silva Method, a way of controlling your own mind in order to be healthier, more successful, and a better problem-solver.

All of these methods followed the same two steps listed above. The reason? They worked.

Two Steps to Change the Polarity of Your Thinking

Read the next line, then close your eyes and repeat it.

**Every day, in every way,
I'm getting more and more positive.**

Now take a deep breath, close your eyes, and repeat that same statement three times.

You have just completed the first step to reprogramming your mind in a more positive direction.

Fact of life: Your thoughts help create your reality. Another fact of life: Your thoughts are the read-out of a programmed computer.

Yes, your brain is a magnificent computer. It has thirty billion neurons, each one functioning like a component of a computer. You turn on your computer by relaxing body and mind. You program your computer by giving it verbal instructions.

You have already started this process. But, in order for it to be dramatically productive, you have to relax more deeply and give verbal instructions that become increasingly more specific.

There are two basic reasons why you must be deeply relaxed for your mental computer to get turned on.

One reason is that your mind won't relax until your body is relaxed. A tense or uncomfortable body is like a small child tugging at its mother's sleeve, saying, "Remember me, remember me."

The second reason is that your right brain hemisphere has to get into the ball game. Even as you read this, your right hemisphere is loafing on the job and all the reading effort is being done by your left hemisphere. As you relax, your right brain hemisphere begins to join the left brain hemisphere. As you deepen your relaxation, your right brain finally stands shoulder to shoulder with your left brain.

"The computer is now turned on."

How to Relax Deeply to Turn On Your Mental Computer

Here are instructions on how to relax your body, then your mind, and how to deepen that relaxation to enable you to program your mental computer.

There are long relaxation techniques and short relaxation techniques.

If you lead a really hectic life, or if you are currently in a period of increased stress, the long relaxation procedures are recommended. However, most people can turn on their mental computer in a few seconds and do not need minutes to get into a state of physical and mental relaxation. For them, the short relaxation techniques work fine.

Here are three long physical relaxation techniques. If you need a period to simmer down, pick one of these:

Three Long Relaxation Techniques

1. Sit in a comfortable position. Close your eyes. Relax your scalp. Relax your forehead. Relax your cheeks, mouth, neck, chest, back, thighs, legs, feet, and toes. Take your time—visualize each body part. Move each part; also mentally "talk" to it and ask it to relax.

2. Sit in a comfortable position. Close your eyes. Take three deep breaths, exhaling slowly after each breath. Now count backwards from 100 to one. Mentally visualize each number before going on to the next.

3. Sit in a comfortable position. Close your eyes and imagine you are in an elevator that is about to descend. It could be an elevator in a department store, in which case you can "hear" the automated voice recite "seventh floor, women's clothes, lingerie," et cetera. When you reach the first floor, you are ready to begin programming your mental computer. Or the elevator can be in a mine shaft. See signs stating each 100 feet down. When you reach 2,000 feet, you are ready to begin mental programming.

Now for a single short technique that is adequate for most people.

A Short Relaxation Technique

1. Sit in a comfortable position. Close your eyes. Take a deep breath and exhale slowly. Do this again. Do this a third time. Now visualize several peaceful scenes you are familiar with. Enjoy each scene as if you were there, being sure to re-create the colors you saw. (See examples below.) You are now ready to program your mental computer.

Relaxing is the art of doing nothing, but we are so used to doing something that we have to do something even to relax.

Note that there is something physical to do in all three long procedures as well as the short one. That provides the physical part of the relaxation. Note also that there is visualization or imagination involved. That provides the mental part of the relaxation. The mind cannot relax easily unless the body is comfortable and not intruding on thoughts.

So these mental pictures are important. They should be taken seriously. Here are some typical scenes that you can use in the short technique:

- A bubbling brook
- Billowing clouds in a blue sky
- A beach with the waves breaking on the shore
- Listening to a symphony
- A flower garden with different flowers and scents
- A rose garden with differently colored roses
- Tropical fish swimming in an aquarium
- A still lake where, at the edge, you can see your reflection

You get the idea. It is not as effective to use hypothetical places such as Cloud 9 or the Garden of Eden. Your body and mind respond best when you have actually seen this place and can mentally reconstruct what it looks like merely by pretending you are there again.

Once you have completed the physical and mental parts of the procedures, whether long or short, you are ready to give yourself life-changing instructions.

You are ready to program your mental computer.

How to Program
Your Mental Computer

Just as there are long and short approaches to relaxation, pro-gramming can take years or it can take seconds.

~Philip grew up in a church-going family. When he left for college, his Sundays changed. Church was forgotten and extracurricular activities took over. After graduating, he entered a retail business. Soon he fell in love and got married.

Now Philip was so involved with making money and family living that nothing could be further from his mind than church. He had no time for spiritual concerns.

So it went for a decade, until Philip was taken seriously ill. He underwent surgery and a long period of recuperation. During this critical time, he lost his business and he lost his wife. He was free to rethink his life.

Some years after this, I met Philip for the first time at a church barbecue. Over frankfurters and corn on the cob, Philip related his story.

"I was too busy making money and having a good time. Little did I know that I was risking a physical shipwreck," he admitted.

When asked what turned him around, he replied, "I read *The Power of Positive Thinking* by Norman Vincent Peale. It lured me back to appreciating those deep and abiding values on which satisfaction in life depends."

Philip is now a business consultant and doing better financially than before, with less stress. He is married to a concert soprano who sings in the church's choir.

Philip had undergone reprogramming. But it took years. His mental outlook was completely different. It went from negative to positive.

You can do it more rapidly. Would you believe in seconds? Here is how:

Exercise to Change Your Mental Outlook

1. Sit in a comfortable position and close your eyes.

2. Take three deep breaths.

3. Visualize several passive scenes.

4. Repeat a positive affirmation three times.

5. Open your eyes, mentally stating, "I am wide awake, feeling more positive than before."

Some Positive Affirmations that Transform Your Thinking

Repeat a positive affirmation three times—fine, but what is a positive affirmation?

An affirmation, no matter what its polarity, is a simple statement of purpose, purposefully stated.

Here are some examples:

**Every day, in every way,
I'm becoming a more and more positive person.**

**Whatever happens today, I will face it with courage
and expect a successful outcome.**

> **I respect myself. I am a capable creator**
> **and problem-solver. I excel.**

These are, of course, positive examples. Negative programming works just as well. But who in the world would want to be more negative in every way; full of fear of failing; and a dismal flop at solving problems?

Using the above examples, you can put together your own positive affirmation. To start with, it should be aimed at positive thinking, self-esteem, and success.

Later, affirmations—the simplest form of programming your mental computer—can be devised to overcome special deficiencies and unwanted habits or personality defects. But at this early stage, positive thinking, self-esteem, and success are our priorities.

For many years, I have seen dramatic transformations in people's polarity with the following dual affirmation:

> **I am frequently a pessimist. I worry.**
> **When I open my eyes,**
> **I will no longer be a pessimist,**
> **I will be an optimist.**
> **I will no longer worry about bad outcomes;**
> **I will expect successful outcomes.**

Use this for three days, three times a day. On the fourth day, change to this:

> **I am no longer a pessimist and worrier.**
> **I am an optimist.**
> **I expect successful outcomes.**

Use this for three days, three times a day. You no longer have to use this for programming your mental computer. You are programmed.

Your thinking will change to a more positive position. Your life will change. Exercise the programming by occasionally remembering the words, no matter what activity you are engaged in: "I am an optimist. I have successful outcomes."

And it is so.

∼

2

Step Off the Treadmill of Limited Money and Limited Love Now

~from Konedda, Druid priest and counselor

*M*y name is Konedda. I am a Druid priest. I have counseled many. I now counsel you."

Thank you, Konedda. Your valued information will guide these pages.

The Druids were priests of the Celtic people, a race that included the Bretons, the Highlanders of Scotland, the Irish, the Welsh, and the Cornish. They idolized the oak tree as a symbol of the strength and prolific aspect of nature. And they were involved with the creation of Stonehenge in Britain, which remains to this day one of the more important legacies of the past. Located on the

Salisbury Plain in southern England, it is considered to be mainly a monument to the rising sun, a marker for eclipses, and a source of other astrological observations.

They also built other stone circles, erected pillars, and created other megalithic shrines, including dolmens to hold their abundance of treasures, especially accumulated knowledge.

One legacy of the past has been lost in the complexity of the present. It is the legacy of abundance. Two ancient cities, lost for centuries, have recently been discovered that illustrate this abundance in breathtaking ways. One is located in Jordan, now hidden by narrow canyons and rock slides but still exhibiting styles of architecture borrowed from the dominant European cultures of the time. It is breathtaking in the vastness of its halls and rooms, all chiseled from the rock cliffs and all adorned with an abundance of time-consuming and time-tested art.

The other ancient city has been recently found in the dense forests of Peru, about fifty miles northwest of Cuzco. Buried for centuries by the vines, trees, and dense undergrowth of the Andes mountains, it was named Machu Picchu and was both the greatest metropolis and strongest fortress of its time. To try to construct an equivalent citadel today would tax the wealth of the entire civilized world.

Neither of these cities are associated with the Druids, but they are examples of how a legacy of abundance such as that of the Druids can remain hidden from us.

The Druids, the Oak Tree, and You

The Druids worshipped the oak tree not only for its strength and abundance of its seed, the acorn, but for the understanding it gave them of the meaning of life.

Life is an endless chain. Should the oak ever be felled, it lives on in the many oaks that grow from its seed. The oak tree was never born and it therefore never dies. So it is with humankind. Life is an endless chain of experiences with no beginning and no end.

And, therefore, with no natural limitations.

But there are unnatural limitations. These are the limitations unnatural to the intelligence that runs the limitless universe but natural to the human mind.

We suffer from unnatural limitations. These limitations are caused by our thoughts. What we believe to be limited becomes limited in our life.

Nobody will argue with the fact that, in this life, we have limited money and limited love. Still, it is not true. Most of us who live this life make it true.

There is no limit to the money anyone can have. But because their name is not Bates, or Forbes, or Perot, or Rockefeller, they think they have been born into a world of limited income and limited wealth.

There is no limit to the love anyone can have. But because when they look in the mirror they don't see a Monroe or a Garbo, a Peck or a Cooper, they think that they have been born into a world of limited mutual attraction, and therefore of limited love.

Suffering from limited money or limited love is needless suffering. Your suffering is caused by your thoughts. Change your thoughts and you change your life. Here is how to make these changes.

How to Profit from a Druid Secret

The Druid priest Konedda was no ordinary person. As a Celt he appreciated the extraordinary capabilities of the Celtic women, who knew how to draw on the limitless power of the Goddess within. She had wisdom, self-confidence, and magical strength.

Today, Celtic music survives and bears more than a hint of that ancient wisdom. In fact, Celts today see in that music a promise of a Celtic tomorrow—a resurgence of Celtic magic and the limitless life that it promises.

As spiritual leaders of the Celts, the Druids were considered to be the magicians and sages of their day. They were the masters of enchantment, the diviners of love. But their essential function was sustaining the prosperity of tribe and land. They did this by what was then considered to be magical means.

However, it was less magic than mental, a means that Jesus had taught centuries earlier but was little perceived and less perpetuated. It was a special use of the mind. Jesus put it this way: Go to the kingdom of heaven within, function within God's righteousness, and all things will come unto you.

Translated into contemporary language, Jesus was saying, in effect: Go within through meditation. Imagine money problems solved, health restored, creative goals reached. And whatever you so imagine will come to pass.

In the days of the Druids, the individual power was looked up to. To share the creative ability of the mind with the common people was to give up your power over them. Of course, today the de-occulting of the occult is well underway. Millions of people, perhaps billions, already know the creative power of thinking.

Why, then, do they not use it? Why do they suffer from lack of money and why do they stifle their desire for love? Yes, I am talking to you.

The answer lies in the hypnotic power of the material world to monopolize your senses and to program your consciousness.

Limited space and limited time spawns in you limited thoughts and a limited life. Thoughts of limitation bring you limited love and limited ability. You build a prison of limitation for yourself. In the next five minutes, you will find that the prison door was never locked.

You will open it and emerge into a bright new world of untold riches and fabulous love. This will happen because two quick demonstrations will convince you that your mind is capable of more than you thought. You will change your mind about your mind.

This will start with your mind's control over your body. By seeing this happen in real life, you will open the way for your mind to continue its creative ability beyond your body—to your bed and to your bank account.

Two Exercises that Begin to Open the Door

The first exercise involves your arms. Read the instructions twice, then do it.

Exercise #1

Standing, hold both arms straight out in front of you, palms down, your arms parallel to the floor. Close your eyes. Imagine a heavy shopping bag full of groceries hanging from your right wrist. Imagine it being so heavy that you can hardly hold it. Imagine a big balloon pulling up on your left wrist. Make these mental pictures real. After a few seconds, open your eyes.

Read the instructions a second time. Done? Okay. Stop reading here, and do the exercise.

When you closed your eyes, your arms were at the same height. Now the right arm is lower than the left. Why?

The second exercise is best done seated. Read the instructions twice, then do it.

Exercise #2

Turn your head to the left as far as it will comfortably go and remember how far that was. Close your eyes and imagine that you are able to turn your head much farther than you did. Open your eyes and once again turn your head to the left.

Read the instructions a second time. Stop reading here. Do it.

When you turned your head to the left for the second time, it went a bit farther than the first time. Why?

The answer to both "whys" is: Your mind controls your body.

Do you realize what this means?

For starters, it means that you can make yourself sick and you can make yourself well. It means, too, that you can tap all the energy you need for whatever you need to do. It means you can develop skills and talents you never believed could be yours.

As a next step, you will learn that science has found that all our minds are connected to each other. That concept is indeed a quantum leap for the mind.

Do you realize what this means?

Eventually, on these pages, you will learn that thought is creative energy and that wealth, also being energy, can be created by thought as well.

And do you realize what this means?

Why the Poor Get Poorer and the Rich Get Richer

～Everett was fortunate to go to college but unfortunate in not being able to finish. The son of a Kentucky farmer who had saved enough in the good years to be able to afford his son's tuition for a little while, Everett found himself back on the farm after a year in a state university.

His taste of higher education made him bitter, and it gave him a feeling of inferiority. It intensified the belief that this was a world of

"haves" and "have-nots," and that he was destined
to remain in the latter group.

For a while, he drove a school bus, but was
found to have liquor on his breath one working
day and was discharged. He used his earnings to
buy a used truck and help farmers with their
cartage. His mother died and, one year later,
his father did too. Now he was too busy with
the farm to earn trucking money. He lived on
his own produce and sold the surplus.

How is Everett doing now? "Haven't heard.
I don't believe he has the money for postage."

The poor get poorer because the hypnotic effect of the limitations of the material world are just too dominant to be considered beatable.

～Take, by contrast, Eugene. He was born in
Westchester County, New York, a wealthy suburb
of New York City. His father, a bank vice president,
talked money at home constantly. The family
enjoyed all the luxuries they wanted, traveled
abroad with Eugene and his sister, and sent them
both to the best universities.

When Eugene graduated, he disappointed his
father by refusing to take a job in that same bank.
He was sure that a life of abundance was his for
the asking, free of paternal supervision. Instead,
he joined an investment firm. His optimistic
attitude won him client after client. His choice
of investments proved magical. Everything he
touched seemed to turn to gold.

Eugene married and lived in Southampton,
Long Island, where his family grew to five
children. His father remained paternal, but
Eugene let his advice bounce off him. He was
his own entrepreneur and the world had no
limitations. The last I knew about Eugene
was seeing his name on the Fortune 500 list.

The rich get richer because they do not believe in any limitations in the material world.

Poor or Rich—
the Choice Is Yours

The Druids were rich. They were rich because they made the choice to be rich and, once they made that choice, they knew how to manifest richness. They taught one another but seldom divulged their mental methods to outsiders. Today all we really know is that they attracted gifts from persons of every rank.

Each knew their relationship to the abundant universe early in life. This basic identity, when formed early in life, can remain essentially unchanged throughout life. The poor stay poor. The rich stay rich. Riches can be attracted to you in the form of friendships, joy, belongings, and, yes, even cash.

Occasionally, a life trauma of major proportions can alter these deep subconscious beliefs. A loss, an illness, a divorce, an incarceration can make a change in a person's subconscious beliefs in either direction. When the direction is positive, the event is usually referred to as enlightenment, or being "born again." In Japan, it would be called "Satori," in India "Samadhi."

Even a major trauma may not affect a person strongly enough to move him or her from a world of need to a world of plenty. Psychologists recognize a resistance to change. This immobility and preference for the status quo causes such a person to consider the new events as a threat and they attempt to sweep them under the table.

We will assume that you are not such a person or you would not have this book in your hands. We will also assume that nobody with a consciousness of plenty would want to move to a consciousness of need, and that what is now being awaited are the steps you are to take to implement your choice.

Here are those steps. No life trauma. Just pleasant thoughts.

A Simple Procedure to Cause a Shift in Consciousness from Poverty to Plenty

The Hawaiian kahunas, or wise men, knew the power of the mind. They called a level of mind beyond the conscious level the "unihipili." They considered it the Creator within us, the Creator that fills all space and is all-intelligent. Since there is no written source for this, we must rely on those whose research has become most respected and used by Hawaiians today. Such an authority is the late Mary Fukui, who calls the unihipili a "kind of spiritual pipeline to supernatural powers."

The Druids must have known of this pipeline, too. Their "magic" transcended sleight of hand and optical illusion and manifested quite dramatically in material ways.

A breed of New Age scientists today have endorsed this concept and developed ways to harness this spiritual pipeline for personal gain. Conventional scientists have turned their professional backs on inner knowledge obtained subjectively.

A strong bias exists against all knowledge that has not been obtained and tested by standard measurable procedures.

Meanwhile, millions of people, encouraged by their spiritual beliefs or trained by such commercial courses as the Silva Method, are able to tap this supernatural power within through simple relaxation accompanied by special mental communication.

You have already followed the simple step to relax the body and mind outlined in Chapter 1. Prepare now to learn the simple steps that enable you to communicate with the supernatural power within you that we have been calling the Creator.

It is something that has been considered a waste of time. It is forbidden in the conventional classroom. Yet it is the most powerful attribute of the human mind.

It is called daydreaming.

A Similarity Between Nightdreaming and Daydreaming

The encephalogram measures brain pulsations. These pulsations are electrical waves that are a measure of states of consciousness.

Right now your brain waves are probably at a frequency of fourteen to twenty-two per second. If you were to close your eyes and relax, as you did in Chapter 1, chances are you would lower your brain wave frequency to somewhere between seven and fourteen waves per second.

That is called the alpha brain wave frequency. It is at the alpha brain wave frequency that we daydream. It is also at the alpha brain wave frequency that we dream at night.

The active brain wave frequency you are now at is called beta. We start to fall asleep below alpha, at four to seven pulsations per second, called theta, and as our brain waves slow up to below four, at delta, we are in deep sleep.

We do not dream at delta. We do not dream at theta. But during the night, every hour and a half our brain waves become faster and, when they reach alpha, we begin to dream.

These periodic nightdreams have something in common with daydreams. They often turn out to be inspired by the source of infinite intelligence we call the Creator.

Niels Bohr, a physicist who worked for years to discover the nature of matter, received the information he needed to construct the periodic table of elements in a dream. That dream won him the Nobel Prize. The Nobel Prize is, besides the honor, real money. His dream made him rich.

So did a dream of Sir Frederick Grant Banting, who discovered in a dream his laboratory approach for production of insulin. The biographers of Giuseppe Tartini, composer of "The Devil's Sonata," describe how it came to him in a nightdream. In the dream, he handed his violin to the devil to see how he could play. "I heard him play with consummate skill a sonata of such exquisite beauty . . . I felt enraptured." He awoke, picked up his violin, and tried to play the sounds he heard in the dream. The piece he then composed was not as good as he heard in his dream, but it was still the best he had ever done.

Robert Louis Stevenson exploited his dreams in his notable writing career. An example was *Dr. Jekyll and Mr. Hyde,* where a difficult part of the plot—the transformation—came to Stevenson in a dream. This was when Hyde, in the presence of his pursuers, took the powder and underwent the change to Dr. Jekyll.

These nightdreams have something in common with daydreams. They are both the source of creativity. Nightdreams are more spontaneous. Daydreams are more under control and purposeful. Each foreshadows reality.

> ⌒Mary marvelled at what a beautiful day it was and wished she could take her children to the beach. But she did not have any money, not even bus fare. She relaxed and daydreamed about being at the beach and helping the children play in the sand.
>
> A few minutes later, one of her boys came running in. "Hey, Mom, look what we found on the lawn!" It was a ten-dollar bill.

What is there about nightdreams and daydreams that make them both creative?

They are both at the alpha level.

The Amazing Ability You Acquire at the Alpha Brain Frequency

What is there about a brain wave frequency of seven to fourteen cycles per second that makes you change from a creature of circumstances to a *creator* of circumstances?

Science discovered the answer to this question within the past fifty years: At alpha, the right hemisphere gets into the thinking process. Is this important because it doubles the thinking ability? Yes, but that's only a tiny piece of the story. The whole story lies in the world-shaking fact that the right hemisphere is our connection to creativity. That is about as far as science has gone. Are you willing to go one step further with me? All you have to do is agree that creativity must be a characteristic of the creative realm.

Where is the creative realm? Who knows and who cares? What is important is that it is where everything is created—from the material world to you. At the alpha brain frequency, your right brain gets into the ball game. It connects you to where you came from: the source of all intelligence.

Nightdreaming and daydreaming connect you to a source of all information, all answers, all solutions. When explaining this to audiences of business people, I tell them, "You have been doing business with your left brain only. It is like having one arm tied behind your back." That is an understatement. The limitation of having only one arm is nothing compared to having only your left brain.

I took the IQ test necessary to become a member of MENSA, those in the top two percent of the world's human intelligence. I failed. Then I took the Silva Method training, which is one way to get your right brain under your control. I took the IQ test again and easily made the grade. I am now a member of MENSA.

Yes, you can raise your IQ. And . . . you can do much more.

There Are No Limits to the Power of Your Mind to Bring Wealth and Love

How much more can you do?

Well, how much more could you do if you were godlike? That's what you are about to become now. It is so simple that one wonders why it is not taught in universities. Or in high schools. Or even in kindergartens.

We who work with both sides of our brains have given up hope for education. It has a monolithic structure that resists changes. We have not given up hope for science. Philosopher-scientists are leading the way. Other scientists are bound to follow in the next 100 or 200 years.

Let's not wait. Let's take a step right now to put our right brain to work.

In Chapter 1 you practiced relaxing by sitting in a comfortable chair, closing your eyes, and taking three deep breaths. You visualized some peaceful scenes and were ready to give your mental computer reprogramming with positive affirmations.

The reason the affirmations actually reprogrammed your thinking was because by relaxing and visualizing you activated your right brain hemisphere. It joined your already active left brain hemisphere in working for you. You can program your whole brain, but you cannot program half of your brain any more than you can program half of a computer.

You will now use the same procedure to relax and visualize. Once you have relaxed with three deep breaths and visualized peaceful scenes, you will again program your mental computer, but in a different way. You will still imagine and affirm, but with a surprising twist.

What you will do is imagine a person who is your connection to the Creator. Who is this person? You know this person very well, but you have not been on talking terms.

It is your higher self.

our higher self is the first link in a chain of command that goes through angelic beings and ascended masters—via a route that is impossible for the human mind to comprehend—all the way to the Creator. By imagining your higher self, you are acknowledging your willingness to receive help from the Creator through these spiritual channels.

Even if you have been devoted to a particular religion, you have quite likely limited such religious activities to intellectual or left brain approaches. What a difference the right brain makes! You will not be breaking with your religion. You will be maximizing its benefits. Has your religion brought you wealth and love?

It will now.

The Act of Reuniting with Your Higher Self

Although the procedure that you are about to experience is simply accomplished, its results are far from simple. In fact, they are vast.

As you gain the wisdom of your new connectedness, you will experience a new life within you. You will become more aware of your part in creation. You will then be able, with help from the chapters ahead, to take additional steps to become the fullest expression of your higher self and a liberally flowing channel for wealth, health, love, and peace.

A piece of advice as you progress: Refrain from talking about it to others. As you try to describe these spiritual experiences, you will have to reach for words that suffice. You will find that words do not suffice. And as you begin to use the words that come nearest to doing the impossible job, you change the experience to fit the words.

This may cost you some wealth, some health, some love, or some peace. Don't dull these experiences. Keep them pure, poignant, and productive.

What you are about to do now may seem faintly familiar to you. Walter de la Mare described this when he said, "Experience seems to be like the shining of a bright lantern. It suddenly becomes clear in the mind what was already there, perhaps, but dim."

The Druids were not the first to utilize their connection to the higher self. It goes back for millennia. It is a rare memory that surfaces when the individual seeks it. It says to you, "Knock and I will answer."

You are about to knock.

This One Minute Is Priceless to You

Read the instructions that follow and then read them a second or third time, as you will not be permitted to pick up the book once this one-minute procedure has begun.

Exercise to Meet Your Higher Self

1. Sit in a comfortable position, close your eyes, and take three deep breaths.

2. Visualize several peaceful scenes.

continued

ne a person entering the room. It is you, but
feet taller and bathed in white light.

mentally, three times, "I love you
and need your help."

5. Mentally rise. Let there be a mutual embrace.
   Mentally be reseated.

6. End by opening your eyes and affirming
   energetically, "I am wide awake and
   in closer touch with the Creator."

Put the book down and do it.

Now that you have had this experience, it would be best to discontinue reading for a while so that you can let the meaningfulness of the moment sink in. An hour or so should suffice.

A change has taken place in you. It is an internal change that will manifest externally in your circumstances. It is a psycho-spiritual change that is beginning to spread around the world as people ask themselves, "Is there a better way?"

The current resurgence of interest in angels is one indication of this spiritual awakening. Angels are now featured in best-selling books, on magazine covers, and in television shows.

Your higher self is closer to the angelic energies. You are now closer to your higher self. *Quid pro quo:* You are now closer to the angelic energies. And because these angelic energies are, in effect, the hand of the Creator at work . . . I'll let you finish that thought.

How to Make the Flame
Burn Brighter

In the chapters ahead, you will learn how to activate this divine connection for wealth, for love, and for the solution of problems. But meanwhile, the flame you have just kindled needs to be nurtured. Soon it will burn brighter and illuminate your life.

There are two main aspects to this nurturing:

1. Recall with joy the image of your embrace.

2. Keep what you have experienced to yourself.

Recalling the image of your higher self and how you embraced it reinforces the connection. Be secretive about this. Talking about the experience to others dispels the energy and sooner or later the fruit of your spiritual gain will wither on the vine.

As you recall it secretly to yourself, it goes to work for you immediately. You feel better. Your outlook on life improves. And then another thing happens, as sure as there is a law of attraction. You attract to yourself what you need in life, not necessarily what you have been getting, in the way of material comforts and loving relationships.

In Chapter 1, I emphasized the importance of doing good for other people and going that extra step in whatever creative work you do. Your higher self loves you for that, and therefore so does the Creator. Each act of doing good makes the flame you have just kindled grow brighter.

You begin to demonstrate higher wisdom and greater capabilities. In the powerful book *Higher Creativity*,[1] the authors

---

1. Harmon, Willis, Ph.D. and Howard Rheingold. Los Angeles, Calif.: Jeremy P. Tarcher, 1984.

state, "Guidance can be found, and the authority is the most trustworthy possible mentor—one's own higher self." Recalling the experience is fine. But soon you should go one step further. You should relax, invite in your higher self, and have a dialogue. You talk mentally. You listen. What you hear is not a voice that thunders in the room and says, "Now I'm going to tell you what to do." Don't wait for that or you'll wait a long, long time.

What happens takes place immediately. Thoughts come as to what you should do. They seem to be your own thoughts but they are really those of a higher source. You will recognize them as good ideas.

You are right. They're the best.

How to Send Out a Call for More Love and Wealth

We are going to assume that some time has passed and that you have developed a positive ongoing relationship with your higher self.

How much time? Well, it all depends on the individual's earnestness and motivation. The greater, the quicker. But if a serious money problem exists (underline "serious"), *then do not wait. Make your appeal now.* Here is how.

You do not have to relax to appeal for help of any kind. You can use a hand position to take the place of relaxation. However, you must program your mental computer that "when I do this, you do that" ("this" being the hand position and "that" being to send a call for help to the Creator via the higher self).

The hand position used most generally is putting the palms together in prayer. But just like the proverbial person who cries wolf at the slightest fear, this prayer position is possibly no longer as effective as it might once have been.

Any gesture you decide on is acceptable. If you decide on making the V for victory sign, fine. If you decide on putting a forefinger in your ear, once it is programmed, it, too, will work, but it will not be quite as socially acceptable as one I use: Put the index finger and thumb together.

Putting these two fingers together of either hand is imperceptible. Nobody will question you. You can do it walking, standing, seated, even driving a car.

Read these instructions over two or three times until you are familiar with the steps.

Exercise to Program a Hand Position

1. Sit in a comfortable position, close your eyes, and take three deep breaths.

2. Visualize several peaceful scenes.

3. Visualize your higher self—a taller "you" bathed in light. Mentally say, "I love you."

4. End your visualization and bring the thumb and index finger of one hand together.

5. Mentally repeat three times: "Every time I put these two fingers together, of either hand, my mind works at a deeper level of awareness for closer contact with my higher self and my Creator."

6. Open your eyes, mentally stating, "Wide awake."

Now put the book down and do it.

〜Burt is a newspaper photographer. He has been using this two-finger communicating technique for several years. One day, after completing a photographic appointment and driving home, he put his two fingers together and asked his higher self, "Is there another place I should go?"

Within a few seconds he found himself turning right without any apparent reason. The road led to the harbor. As he approached, he saw a boat burning in the water. He parked, took pictures, and got a pretty penny for them.

〜Ginny never enjoyed a lasting relationship. She longed for marriage and children. Before looking at the Internet one afternoon, she daydreamed about meeting the right man. That very time, a man engaged her in conversation . . . that eventually led to marriage.

There are advanced ways to get divine help on the pages ahead. Meanwhile, for more wealth and more love, just put your two fingers together and ask.

〜

3

The Amazing Power of Positive Imaging

⁓*from Panopoulos, Greek naturalist*

*G*reek naturalists, getting their inspiration from the beauty of Greek woods and streams, extrapolated natural characteristics into human life. Nature was at the core of their architecture and at the core of their democracy.

Nature's ways were synchronized with mathematics by Pythagoras, as far back as the sixth century. Nature's ways were reconciled with the art of successful living by Plato. Nature's ways became the ways of the gods by Greek religionists.

The key to this extrapolation of nature to such seemingly diverse areas as mathematics and religion was with the use of mental imagery. Socrates claimed that seeing with the eyes was far less reliable than seeing with the mind.

Plato saw less of a future for humankind in the pursuit of human pleasures than in the pursuit of the Creator's pleasures—making this a better world to live in. In Athens his appeal was: "You, my friend—a citizen of the great and mighty and wise city of Athens—are you not ashamed of heaping up the greatest amount of money and honor and reputation and caring so little about wisdom and truth and the greatest improvement of the soul which you never regard or heed at all?"

His lesson to the Greeks and later to the world was that nature's wealth, a product of the Creator, far exceeds our cash. His concept of society was one of human perfection through the application in life of vision.

Panopoulos lived in Athens, Greece, in the early days of the fourth century B.C. This was a time of transition, when the great city-states were losing their importance. To Panopoulos this was a time of promising transition, when people with imagination could influence changes with limitless possibilities.

Though a city dweller, Panopoulos spent much of his time in nearby wooded hills observing nature. This was one of the reasons why he became a member of Plato's circle of intellectuals. He probably played no small part in supporting Plato's concept of individuals seeking perfection through vision.

Seeing with the Mind
Yields Insight

The Greeks discovered that obtaining fundamental insights was not the monopoly of geniuses but actually a skill that could be learned and developed. Their people looked forward to participating in the state meetings where ideas were expressed toward solving society's problems. Many took time out in advance to meditate about the contributions that they might be able to make at these meetings. What they then expressed at these meetings was the stuff of geniuses—inspired solutions.

Taking time out to be quiet and search for answers is really not time out but rather time in. Consciously or not, you are turning off the outside world and turning on an inner world. This inner world is the source of vision, inspiration, and insight. Why? Because it is your window on infinite intelligence.

We call the spiritual world of the Creator the creative realm. We use "tuning in" as a way of tapping that realm. Are we trespassing? Do we of the physical realm have a right to venture mentally into the spiritual realm?

The measuring stick that we have available to gauge right or wrong is our conscience. How do we feel about going to the spiritual realm within?

Why not do it now and see how you feel about it? Read these instructions twice:

Exercise to Enter the Spiritual Realm

1. Sit in a comfortable chair, close your eyes, and take three deep breaths.

2. Imagine your higher self in front of you, bathed in light.

3. Say "I love you."

4. Be aware of how you feel.

5. Open your eyes, saying mentally, "Wide awake."

Put the book down and do it.

How did you feel while being in the spiritual realm within?

"I felt insulated against stress."

"I felt closer to God."

"It was a feeling of being free."

"There is a peace within that is hard to describe."

"I felt I could overcome all limitations."

These are some of the responses received to that question. Says the *Daily Word*,[1] "I am as free and expansive in my thinking and actions as I allow myself to be."

It appears to be unanimous. The feeling was good. By going within to the spiritual realm, you are not trespassing. In fact, the feeling is so good—good for your health, well-being, peace, and intelligence—that it is quite likely one is remiss by *not* going within.

---

1. Silent Unity, 1901 NW Blue Parkway, Unity Village, Mo. 64065-0001.

Objective and Subjective Uses of the Inner World

Half the world goes within daily. Most of these are people who do so because it is part of their religious practice to meditate. These include Buddhists, Taoists, and Christians.

Not all in these religions meditate, but if you are one who does not go within periodically, a great reward awaits you when you begin to do so. You can enjoy a better life if you periodically go within. This is true in two ways. You can function subjectively or objectively. In either way, the rewards are bountiful.

Let us examine these two approaches. First, the subjective approach to going within. This is the approach where you go within to just be there. This is called passive meditation. It is the most common use of meditation.

A few minutes just being in the spiritual realm is a restorative tonic. It is like going to an energy bank and making a withdrawal. When you end your meditation, you feel enriched in many ways.

Then there is the objective approach to going within. This is the approach where you go within to do something while you are there—to either pray or to use your imaging ability to "see" some problem solved. This is called dynamic meditation.

I was invited by the Theosophical Society to introduce dynamic meditation in their headquarters at Adyar, India. This was like carrying coals to Newcastle, as India is probably the birthplace of meditation.

As my lectures and practice sessions proceeded, with attendees using the meditative state to "see" their life as they would prefer it to be, I was asked, "Sir, are we not storming the gates of heaven?"

"Yes," I replied. "But is it not about time we did?"

Nobody is advised to give up passive meditation in favor of dynamic meditation. But a mix of both works well. Here is a classic example of the creative aspect of dynamic meditation:

～A waiter, who walked from his apartment to the restaurant where he worked daily, passed a beautiful mansion surrounded by gardens. He never failed to stop and admire this dream home on his way to work and on his way back. Admiring its beauty, he would close his eyes and picture himself living there. Opening his eyes, he would continue his walk in the "real" world.

One evening, the elderly lady he was serving in the restaurant said to him, "I see you stop and admire my home daily; how would you like to live there?"

Nearly dropping his tray, he stammered, "What do you mean?"

"I'm too old to take care of it, so I'm retiring to Florida," she continued. "I want the house to be in the hands of one who appreciates it. I think you are such a one."

The waiter was soon the owner of the house he saw in his daydreams—in his dynamic meditations.

Write Your Own Ticket
While in the Creative State

Just going within—as you have learned to do by merely closing your eyes, taking a few deep breaths, and visualizing passive scenes—is a therapeutic act. It helps body, mind, and spirit.

But taking that extra step of visualizing or imagining a benefit to yourself or somebody else not only helps your body, mind, and spirit, it also helps another person, perhaps many other persons, and perhaps the world.

If such imagined thoughts are positive and do not cause a problem for somebody else, there is every likelihood they will happen just as you imagined them. To entertain such positive pictures while relaxed is to do your duty as a co-creator—a partner with the Creator.

What are the limits? There are no limits. Yes, you can write your own ticket by daydreaming.

What has imaging got to do with your suddenly acquiring a new car?

What has holding your two fingers together got to do with a solution to a desperate problem?

What has a controlled positive daydream got to do with your enjoying an increase in youthful energy and vitality?

Nothing, from what you have been taught in school or in church. But, from the standpoint of a new science—everything. One is the cause. The other is the effect. The imaging, the finger position, the controlled daydream are the causes. The new car, the new solution, the new vitality are the effects. The way your life unfolds for you is a cause-effect relationship.

The mind is creative. The way you use it shapes your life. If this comes as news to you, it is good news and just in time.

Your mind and your health have a cause-effect relationship. Do something about it.

Your mind and your bank account have a cause-effect relationship. Do something about it.

Your mind and the fruitfulness of your human relationships have a cause-effect relationship. Do something about it.

The "something" in all three cases involves positive mental imaging while relaxed. Let's take a deeper look at this word "positive."

To Think Positively Is to Be Part of the Solution, Not Part of the Problem

Humans are learning to use more of their minds. It is a slow process, but none too soon if the battlefields are to be neutralized, the jails and hospitals emptied, the forests preserved, and planet Earth saved.

⟋Carole took a mind-training course because she was in a rut. She felt that her job was boring and her social life nil. Within two weeks of mentally "seeing" herself in the right job for her and with the right man, Carole had found a challenging position and was going steady with a man she eventually married.

⟋Martin took a similar mind-training course. He was the local head of a manufacturing company sales staff but competition was getting the upper

hand. In the following weeks, he relaxed and
daydreamed about increased sales. Concurrently
he began to develop new ways to outsell
competitors. Later that year he was elevated to
a regional sales management appointment.

Carole solved her own personal problem. Martin not only
solved his own personal problem but, in the process, solved a
problem for everybody in the manufacturing company.

Where do you start? Do you daydream to create a better
love life for yourself or a bigger bank account?

The answer lies in how I began this short course that you
hold in your hand. I had you begin not by helping yourself but
by helping others. This establishes you as a co-creator. Once
known to the Creator as a co-creator, you become more eligible for creative support on whatever level—for planet Earth or
yourself.

I am advising you, in order to change your life for the better, to think not only positively but also POSITIVELY.

To do so is to harness the greatest power of your own mind.
Besides having a visible means of support, you then acquire an
invisible means of support also. Asked to describe what this
means, I throw up my hands. Your invisible means of support
is indescribable.

It is like sitting at the right hand of God.

One Daydream that Provides You with a Winning Ticket

The tale is told of a man named Smith who relaxed and spoke
to the Creator about his problem. "My business is failing.

Only winning a lottery will save me. Please cause me to be a lottery winner."

Nothing happened. He was getting desperate. He tried again. "My business has now failed. I am at a loss as to how to survive. Only a lottery win can solve my financial problem."

Again nothing happened. Smith made a third attempt. "Dear Creator, now my wife has left me. What shall I do?"

Before he could end his session, a voice boomed in his head. "Smith: Please buy a lottery ticket."

Don't make the same mistake of expecting to win the lottery without making the first step of buying the ticket. You are now being asked to buy a spiritual lottery ticket. Contrary to the usual lottery ticket, spiritual lottery tickets are sure winners. Your lottery ticket, which will place you in line to receive immense personal rewards, is to go to your relaxed state and visualize help for others first.

The Problems of the World that Need Your Help

The kinds of help that you can provide by relaxed daydreaming are endless. But you do not have to solve them all. Why not recall what has touched you the most and select one or two to devote your creative energy toward and earn your spiritual lottery ticket? Here are ten examples to trigger your memory:

- Shortage of food in North Korea
- People living off the Manila garbage dump
- Prostitution among young girls in Thailand

- Unrest in Bosnia
- Ethnic conflicts
- Terrorism in Ireland
- Conflict in Israel
- Rising crime in a big city
- Corruption in local, state, or federal government
- Gangs disrupting a neighborhood

Note that these are specific examples of general problems. You might have a specific example of violence on television to use in your relaxed daydreams. Or, you might wish to use a specific example of the prevalence of the AIDS virus in some activity or location.

Then there are ways to help particular individuals or families. You would visualize your neighbor with a runaway son back home, or a sick relative recovered, or a high school graduate you know being admitted to an affordable college.

Any problem for which you can imagine the solution is a problem that you can help to end.

No matter what you choose to help the Creator with, it is a valid price to pay for your lottery ticket—and they are all solved by the same procedure.

How to Help Solve Any Problem No Matter Where It Is

The procedure is one that you already are at least partly familiar with. Here it is. Read it over two or three times so that you are sure you know the steps.

Exercise to Solve Any Problem

1. Sit in a comfortable chair, close your eyes, and take three deep breaths.

2. Visualize some peaceful scenes.

3. Deepen your relaxation by counting backward from ten to one.

4. Visualize or imagine the problematic situation that you have chosen to help correct, keeping the mental picture dark and dismal.

5. Visualize or imagine the situation corrected, making the mental image bathed in light.

6. Open your eyes, saying "wide awake." Feel good that the solution image is on its way.

Now put the book down and do it.

The feeling of helping with a problem is a positive feeling. It stirs up one's motivation to work, if you can call it that, on other problems. As you do more and more, the larger becomes your own eligibility for personal rewards.

Distance is no factor. The problem can be on the other side of the world. Problem size is no factor. It can involve one individual or the entire population of a country. Time is no factor. The problem may appear to be a perpetual one, but it can disappear as quickly as the Berlin Wall came tumbling down.

The amazing power of positive imaging was never publicized on front pages or cover stories. Yet it has always existed.

Inventors, artists, and architects are the most obvious examples of its use to create. But it goes much further than that.

The chair you are sitting in would not exist if some furniture designer did not "see" it with the mind's eye first. Then he or she sketched it, and carpenters could construct it. The clothes you are wearing right now would not exist if some designer did not "see" them first. Only then could the sketches be drawn and the patterns made. The building you are in right now would not be here either, had not it been "seen" by the architect. Only then could it be rendered in perspective, plans and elevations drawn, bids solicited, and construction begun.

Entire civilizations have sprung from mental images. Greek myths about their own history evolved from the imagination. Greek art did likewise. Men like Panopoulos had vivid imaging faculties that set new standards for creativity and beauty. A revolution in philosophy was pioneered by Socrates' imaginative and creative mind; it brought about a return to moral principles.

Adopting Socrates' principles was not creative. Being influenced in art by Polygnotus' murals was not creative. One might say that the Greek influence in the world began to wane when action preceded by imagination gave way to imitation.

Imagination is tapping the Creator's creativity.

Maintaining contact with the Creator daily is the key to leading an inspired life.

How to Keep in Touch with Your Creativity

Keeping in contact with creativity is the ultimate answer to enjoying a life boundless in love and riches.

So far on these pages we have supplied a number of ways to contact the Creator. These have included:

- Doing good for others
- Imaging and loving your higher self
- Programming and using the two-finger method
- Imagining the world's problems being solved
- Imagining other individuals' problems being solved

Keeping in touch with the Creator involves all of these procedures. The more relaxing and the more creative and positive visualizing a person does, the more "lucky" he or she will be. That person will meet the right members of the opposite sex, find the right friend to influence some needed change in a situation, get the right decision from a judge, invest in the right securities, and enjoy the fruits of what appears to be his or her own thinking but is really emanating from a divine source.

The more you are able to keep in touch with the Creator, the more productive your life will be of comfort, pleasure, ecstasy, and health.

This fact is realized more in Asia than in America. There are thousands of temples throughout Japan, sometimes hundreds in a single city. In Thailand practically every homeowner has a miniature shrine where daily offerings are made. In India, holy men are everywhere and even cattle are considered representatives of the Creator.

In the West—in America and Europe especially—we are too busy to think of the Creator. Only when material activities slow up on weekends do people allow their thoughts to turn to the fact that there is a Creator. On Saturday, the temples are used, and on Sunday, the churches. Even then, the thoughts of many who attend services are more on seeing who is there and being seen, on listening to the leader's thoughts rather than to their own, on reading and singing, on sitting and rising. For many, prayers are far from sincere and largely perfunctory.

I am not advocating non-attendance. I am advocating a more meaningful attendance. You do this by being in mental touch with the Creator through all of the standard rituals.

Convert the prayers, sermons, and psalms into conscious love for the Creator. If you were the Creator, wouldn't you pay more attention to worshippers who paid more attention to you?

Adopting a Special Way to Be Closer to the Creator

There is no more positive thought than a thought of the Creator. And the power of positive thinking is no more dramatically rewarded. Half the world's population has an interesting and effective technique for accomplishing this. It helps to overcome the dominance of our thoughts on the activity of the moment.

If you were to put this book down now and start thinking about the Creator in loving terms, you would be enhancing your connection to the realm from which divine help is assured. But there's a catch.

The phone will ring. Or there'll be a knock on the door. A child will cry for attention. The water will boil. Or you will look at the clock and see that it is time for . . . .

What half the world's population does is to get in the habit of repeating the Creator's name—over and over without ceasing—

all day long. In India, it is Rama, Rama, Rama. In Moslem countries, it is Allah, Allah, Allah.

It is practically impossible to follow suit in English speaking countries, that is, the largely Judeo-Christian world. The reason is that repeating the name of God is like swearing. "For God's sake, stop that." "God, isn't this awful!" "God, what a bore!" "God, when will this end!"

Even the name Jesus Christ has become a swear word. "Jesus, what a hot day!" "Jesus Christ, will you quit!" Jesus this and Jesus that.

The word "abba" means father. It is used in English churches as a title of honor. However, when capitalized—Abba— it is from the New Testament and means God (Mark 14:36).

Try saying it aloud now. Hear how easily it falls off the lips. This is not a requirement, but it is an asset in your spiritual connection. It helps you to stay "on the line" with the Creator.

You can program the meaning of "Abba" into your mental computer. And you can program the tendency to repeat multiple times during your busy day without interfering with your activities. Here is how.

Read these instructions two or three times; you may substitute the word "Creator" for the word "God" if you wish.

Exercise to Program "Abba" Into Your Computer

1. Sit in a comfortable chair, close your eyes, and take three deep breaths.

2. Mentally repeat three times, "Abba means God to me."

3. Then mentally say, "I want to repeat Abba many times each day and I am going to repeat Abba many times each day."

4. Add mentally, "Whenever I think of the name Abba, I will remember it is the name of God."

5. Open your eyes, mentally saying, "Wide awake."

If you are confident that you can remember these steps, put the book down and do it.

Positive or Negative Thinking— A Continuous Effort

Mental programming is evidenced by daily habits. We tend to react the same way to a repeated stimulus or event. Habits are programmed both physically and mentally.

A golfer whose drive is plagued by slices is in the habit of driving the ball that imperfect way. He is programmed by grip and stance to slice. He won't stop slicing the ball until he re-programs himself to drive differently by correcting the physical stroke and practicing these corrections until the new stroke has been programmed. Then he must program himself mentally to expect to drive without a slice.

An older unmarried daughter who has seen her three younger sisters marry has programmed herself toward being a spinster. Look at her. She is even beginning to walk and talk like one. If she wants a family life of her own, she has to change that physical programming in her walk and talk. She also has to program herself mentally to expect a man in her life.

Why has that entrepreneur failed in business three times when others have prospered in those same lines? Answer: Programming a poor self-image. Exactly what specific programming may be difficult to identify but we would bet on programming in his youth that affected his self-image. Can you just hear his mother yelling at him: "Stupid!" And his father: "Clumsy!" And his teacher: "Wrong!" And his classmates: "Beat it!"

His physical programming would be along the lines of programming to change bad business habits, like to stop incurring a high overhead or stop economizing on the quality of the product or service.

This entrepreneur must then program a more positive self-image by daydreaming that he is a successful tycoon or holding other mental images that show him to be a genius in his work. And so it will be.

Motivational experts recommend that associating with positive people helps you to become more positive yourself. One discipline recommends that you observe the mannerisms of successful people and imitate them. I am not opposed to this, but I am more in favor of you observing *your* mannerisms, *your* speech, *your* thoughts.

Mannerisms include your standing posture—is it erect? Your walking posture—do you walk like a loser or a winner? Your facial expression—is it glum or jovial?

Change your body's standing and walking posture to that of a victor and you help yourself move to the winning side.

Change your thoughts from seeing the glass half empty to seeing the glass half full and life becomes fuller.

Change your facial expression to a frequent smile and life becomes rosier.

"Put a smile on your face" has been an age-old instruction for positive thinking. Recently, psychologists recognized the efficacy of this. They found that by smiling, you caused internal changes similar to what exists when you are joyous. They now recommend a smile as the antidote for being "down in the mouth."

When smiling changes your internal environment, it also causes changes in your exterior environment. People respond more acceptably to a smiling face than a glum face. Things go better for you.

Try it today.

How to Get Help from Nature in Improving Your Lot in Life

Ancient Greeks who became creators of that impressive culture frequently received inspiration by being observant of nature.

Aphrodite, their goddess of love and beauty, was conceived as the procreator of nature's lavish beauty and life's ability to reproduce itself in the plant and animal world. Roots breaking through rock obstacles, the strength of the wind, and the irresistible force of the tides were the inspiration for their concept of Apollo.

Nature's lines were adopted in their columns and other architectural motifs. The Colossus of Rhodes, inspired by tall, stately trees, was a statue of Apollo some 120 feet high set at the entrance to the Rhodes harbor about 280 B.C.

Today, we are becoming more and more separated from the Creator by our separation from nature. Skyscrapers, made of concrete and steel, are no source of energy and life to us like groves of trees and growing grass are.

The programming to activate a connection to the Creator via the right brain hemisphere can be assisted by nature. To get the most out of a walk through the park or across a lawn, attune your mind to the life force within the plants, bushes, trees, and blades of grass. Be aware of their support of you, not just by bearing your weight but by sharing their energy with you and by proclaiming to you, via sight, sound, and smell, their own connection to the Creator.

Besides taking a good, brisk walk through nature's world, it is also good to take there what Phyllis Diller calls "a good brisk sit." What better place to sit, close your eyes, take three deep breaths, and "see" your higher self bathed in white light? What better place than on a log, in a grassy green, or by a running brook to relax for a few seconds, take a few deep breaths, and love the Creator?

You will discover the love is mutual.

Mental Housecleaning as a Prerequisite to Positive Thinking

When you contemplate nature, you temporarily absent yourself from a world of obstacles to positive thinking. Some of these obstacles are a messy house, a complicated job, and a tendency to use negative words in everyday conversation.

You can program a sort of mental housecleaning by being aware of these various pressures on you to think limitedly and pessimistically.

How about the messy house? Relax and daydream about cleaning the hall closet, the garage, the attic, the basement, and any other area that is other than orderly. You will find by repeating this daydream a few times that you will not be able to tolerate those overladen shelves or unseemly piles of belongings. Gradually you will find time to clear this mess and that pile. It will be not only a physical housecleaning, but a mental one.

Next the job. How do you keep a job from getting you down, especially when the more you do, the more there appears to do? And your supervisor blasts you for no good reason? And just when you get things down to an easier routine, changes are made to disrupt it?

This is as bad as a messy house in its effect on your thoughts and attitudes. It also requires mental housecleaning to combat its effects on your ability to think positively and therefore get help from the other side.

Just as you relaxed and "saw" yourself cleaning the house, place by place, you need to relax and "see" your job getting more orderly.

Use only one daydream at a time. Perhaps the first would be to "see" yourself happy on the job. Next, you would daydream about having the job easily completed by closing time. Then, the supervisor with a smiling face; and next, your own ability to change as the routine changes.

As you daydream in this manner, you are enjoying a mental housecleaning from the job point of view. Persevere with desire, expectation, and belief, and these daydreams will come true.

Finally, be aware of your language. Language is a habit. We do not think of every word we say before we say it, any more than we think of every separate step we take before we walk. To break the habit of using self-limiting and negative words, we need once again to resort to reprogramming via relaxed imaging and positive mental affirmations.

We are told that in the beginning was the word, meaning that the word was creative. It was the start of the Creator's creation of the material universe.

I have a sneaking suspicion that before the word, there was something else—a laugh. Be that as it may, the word is still there and it is still creating.

Take the word "try." We hear it so often. "I will try to do it." "I will try to be there." "I will try to win."

We will venture to say that whoever said "try" did not do it, did not get there, and did not win. When you say "try" you are giving yourself permission to fail. It is better to say "I'll do it," "I'll be there," "I'll win." By using more affirmative words, the mind gets the message. It then sets its priorities accordingly. Creativity is activated. You succeed.

Many people need a kick in the "can'ts." By using the word "can't," they are making a self-fulfilling prophecy. Say "I can't" and you really can't, even though there is every likelihood you could have.

As you can see, a giant step in mental housecleaning is the reprogramming of everyday speech to be more positive.

Let us now use words to reprogram our use of words. Here is how. Read these instructions several times before doing it.

Exercise to Reprogram Our Use of Words

1. Relax in a comfortable chair. Close your eyes. Take three deep breaths and visualize some peaceful scenes.

2. Repeat mentally several times: "I am aware of the limiting words I use. I understand they affect my life. Since I want a better life, I will now use better words. I now use words that are positive and creative."

3. Open your eyes, mentally saying, "Wide awake and using more positive words than before."

Now put the book down and do it.

Some of our speaking habits are so ingrained that you may still find yourself using an occasional "I can't" or similar self-restricting terms. The above daydreaming session should be repeated if your improvement is not complete.

In a future chapter, we will cover the words we use to make us sick or in pain. The mind runs our life, especially our body's life. With the Creator being our source of life, everything we do to activate our right brain's connection to the Creator becomes a step in the direction of ideal day after ideal day.

～

4

How to Exit Endarkment and Enter Enlightenment

⁓from Takapoosha, Native American sachem

The exposure of Americans to the American Indian today is far removed from what it was in pioneer days. Then it was largely polarized into the killer and the killed. The Indians became the defenders of their native land against the white newcomers.

To the white newcomers, the Indians were obstacles to survival. Kill them, they thought, or be killed by them.

Today, we recognize that the Indians were not the bad guys they were seen as then. In fact, the roles now appear to many to be reversed, as the Indian philosophy becomes clear to us—illustrating a more enlightened civilization than we assumed. They worshipped the Great Spirit as the Creator.

The Indians were more attuned to nature than the white newcomers. The mountain lion selects one bison to attack, usually a weaker one, to feed the family of lions. Similarly, the Indian hunters killed only enough buffalo to feed their tribe members.

The earth was treated with respect. If trees were cut down, trees were replanted. If crops were cultivated, the soil was later permitted to restore itself.

Some tribes were more in tune with nature than others. The chiefs of the leading tribes were called sachems. The Algonquins and the Wampanoags were such tribes. Their sachems used great wisdom in the administration of their people. So great was this wisdom that many sachems were considered godlike. Certainly they had learned how to exit the dark ages and bring an enlightened consciousness to their people.

The last sachem of the Rockaway tribe of Indians was Takapoosha. His grave is unmarked on Long Island, having lived in the eighteenth century as the white settlers arrived. At his death, a cypress tree was planted at his gravesite and the area became a burial ground for dignitaries both among the settlers and his tribe, so respected was he by all.

Takapoosha warned his people that they would have to change their lifestyle with the advent of their new neighbors and they would have to rise to new levels of personal enlightenment in order to live out their days with peace and dignity. He reminded them of the teachings handed down through the tribe's elders where oneness with nature and with all life was emphasized.

In the previous chapter, we recommended closeness to nature as an asset toward the positive thinking so necessary to becoming closer to the Creator. In this chapter, we will take a larger view of Nature and begin to see it as so important an aspect of the Creator that it deserves a capital "N."

The Nature of the Universe

There was a pilot who had flown some of the most dangerous combat missions over Japan for two years in World War II. His attitude all through this danger was, "Nothing will ever happen to me." Nothing did. He returned to the United States without a scratch.

Then he started work as a flight instructor. He had a nickname for his students. He called them "Little Killers." Then one day they lived up to the nickname. They killed him. It is almost unheard of for a student pilot to make a serious enough mistake to kill himself and his instructor. But he had given this student the name, the game, and the opportunity—and it was done.

One day a plane was ready to land in Honolulu, but the crew could not get the landing gear to work. The plane had to wait until the runway was foamed so it could land more safely on its belly. Nobody was hurt, but a passenger later related that the movie shown aboard that flight involved defective landing gear. How could 300 relaxed passengers, all holding such a problem in their mind, not create it?

Some years ago, an atomic physicist received a Nobel prize in physics for discovering a new subatomic particle. In accepting the award at a public ceremony, he stated, "I wondered if that particle was there before I started looking for it." He was inferring that, by imagining that it was there, he created it.

Scientists are beginning to study the energy of consciousness. They can measure it and focus it, but they still do not admit they can create with it. One cannot blame scientists for moving slowly and surely. They need to use the scientific method. They need to observe protocol. They need to publish their findings.

How would you like to be a scientist today and be working at the frontier of matter, where particles end and only systems of energy and intelligence exist? You would be in a real dilemma. You would have to record unscientific matters in a scientific way.

When you discovered intelligence in space, how would you report that discovery without making it sound like you discovered the Creator? What scientific words are there to cover a source of creativity, ingenuity, and intelligence in presumably empty space?

Go one step beyond the bounds of conventional paradigms and your professional reputation would be at stake. Research grants would dry up. Publishers would turn their backs on you. So you would choose not to go that one step beyond. You would not take such a serious risk.

We are now going more than one step beyond. We are going to bless the universe and in turn invite a blessing on us by the Creator.

Were NASA to sponsor the trip we are about to take, it would involve billions of dollars and years of time. But we are not going by space shuttle. We are going by consciousness. We are going to marry our consciousness to Universal Consciousness. By acknowledging the nature of the universe as energy, we are going to bring it energy in the form of light energy, the energy of consciousness, and love energy. We will travel to the limits of this galaxy and back. It will bring us a potential fortune, but cost us nothing.

And it will take only minutes.

A Far Out Way to Greet the Creator

Only by enlisting superhuman intelligence can we rise above our present life status. This superhuman intelligence, once enlisted, manifests through us. We become super loved, super wealthy, superman or superwoman. I am talking about you. I am also talking about the Creator as the only source of superhuman intelligence.

Relax and daydream in a controlled way. It is so easy it is laughable. Somebody once said, "God is not so much denied as crowded out." We are just too busy to daydream.

If you do not find time to daydream in a controlled and positive way, you are on your own. And all that can be said is "Tough"! Your life can become, as Shakespeare wrote, "A tale told by an idiot, full of sound and fury, signifying nothing."

Are you ready to bless the universe and in turn be blessed with superintelligence?

Read these instructions over several times until you are sure you have the hang of it.

Exercise to Become Closer to the Creator

1. Sit in a comfortable chair, close your eyes, take three deep breaths, and visualize several peaceful scenes.

2. Mentally picture the room you are in. Fill it with light. Love it.

3. Imagine you are looking down from above at the building you are in. Surround it with light. Send your love to it.

4. Higher still. Imagine you see your town or city. Surround it with light and love.

5. Higher still. All of the United States. Light and love.

6. Higher still. Planet Earth. Light and love.

7. Finally, the whole galaxy. Light and love.

8. Feel the light and love reflected back at you. Bring it home the way you came—solar system, Earth, the United States, your town, your building, your room.

9. Open your eyes. Mentally say, "Wide awake and closer to the Creator."

Now put the book down and do it.

Leo Tolstoy wrote, "Everybody thinks of changing humanity; nobody thinks of changing themselves." You have just changed yourself. You have an expanded consciousness. You are no longer merely a New Yorker, a San Franciscan, or a Chicagoan. You are a universal person.

Whereas the previous controlled daydreaming trips you have taken to reprogram yourself can be advantageously repeated occasionally for reinforcement, the cosmic trip you have taken need not be taken again. It has accomplished its purpose.

Changes for the better will begin to happen in your life, starting now.

You will wonder why nobody has told you about this before—not your parents, not your teachers, not your church or synagogue leaders.

There could be one of two reasons for this: Either they never heard about it themselves, or they experienced it and realized that it takes a period of preparation first.

Your period of preparation has been the work prescribed in the previous chapters. It is all sequential. You have to crawl before you walk before you run.

Now you are ready to run.

Letting Sunlight into Your Life

One change you will begin to notice in your daily feelings is a warmer feeling toward other people, toward animals, and toward other forms of life.

If you had an aversion to spiders, you might find this has lessened. If you were afraid of dogs, you might think more kindly toward them. You might even start watering plants that others had been taking care of before.

These are all minor indications that, by becoming closer to the Creator, you become more aware of the unity of all life.

An animal trainer named J. Allen Boone wrote a book years ago called *Kinship With All Life.*[1] Training animal stars for Hollywood, he was assigned a dog named Strongheart. For the first time in his life, he wrote, there was an animal that he could not get to respond to him. He could not get to first base with Strongheart. It was not that Strongheart was a slow learner. He was a non-learner. Strongheart was apparently just an independent dog.

Then, late one day, Boone was resting on a grassy knoll. After hours of frustration with Strongheart, now on a leash beside him, Boone looked with admiration at the beautiful sunset. Then he saw that the dog was also looking at the sunset. His animosity toward the dog melted. After all, a dog that sees the beauty in a sunset cannot be all that bad.

The next day Strongheart was a different dog. He did everything he was told to do. Once the poorest, he became the best pupil Boone ever had.

This came as a blow to Boone. What had happened? It was important to his success for Boone to understand why the transformation in this dog had taken place. All he could put his finger on was the sunset. Recalling the incident, he relived how he had felt. He remembered sort of forgiving the dog as they watched the sunset together. He remembered feeling a closeness to the dog—almost a kinship.

Could that be it? Boone set off to the mountains, in the east of the state, where he heard that Indians were able to ride wild horses. He was taken by the Indians to where these wild horses were. As Boone watched, an Indian bowed his head, then

---

1. Harper & Row Publishers: New York, 1954.

walked to a wild horse. To Boone's amazement, the horse permitted the Indian to mount and ride.

When the Indian returned, Boone asked him what he did when he bowed his head. "I visualized the horse. Loved him as a brother. And asked him for permission," was the reply. Boone was then able to repeat the "impossible" act.

Boone then tells how he met rattlesnakes on the way home but talked lovingly to them and they let him pass. At home shaving, a fly bothered him and he told it lovingly to sit on the sill. And it did! He got to know the fly well. He could touch him. He gave him the name Freddie. Freddie became a household pet.

Boone writes that it "became [easier] to recognize him as a fellow expression of the Mind of the Universe . . . . We are members of a vast cosmic orchestra in which each living instrument is essential to the complementary and harmonious playing of the whole."

Does Boone now sound like a man in the dark? He became enlightened, thanks to his experience with Strongheart. And Strongheart went on to become a Hollywood star.

You Become Enlightened by Helping Others to Become Enlightened

Do you help others by having them take the cosmic trip you just took? A waste of time. They did not go through the preliminaries that you did, which are a prerequisite for success. There are other ways to help them, and the more you help them, the more you help yourself.

Sean was the son of an intelligent and aware couple. Several times his fifth grade teacher had sent notes home complaining of Sean's combativeness in class and criticizing his homework habits. Parental talks made no change in Sean's school life. Next came a request by the teacher for a conference.

"Sean is just not the student type, I guess," replied his mother when the teacher had finished her report.

"I think he agrees with that," offered the teacher. "And that may be his problem. He has a low self-esteem. His behavior to the other children appears to be defensive even though he has no reason to be."

The parents perked up. They looked at each other and nodded. "We think you have put your finger on the cause. We know just what to do," promised the father.

For the next several evenings, they used their controlled daydreaming. Each went to the relaxed level and saw Sean ten feet tall, towering over his classmates, symbolic of a new feeling of self-confidence and self-esteem. Then they had Sean relax and daydream about himself. They led him through mental movies of making a touchdown, leading a school parade, winning a spelling bee.

In a month, the teacher wrote another note. "Sean's improvement is spectacular. What did you do?"

They decided not to tell her.

But I will tell you what you can do.

Sean's parents had previously done for themselves what they did for Sean. You must help yourself first. Then you can help others with your own daydreaming, even if these others are miles away. You have already shown your capability and willingness to do good for others by following instructions in Chapter 1. You have the priority now in programming for your own personal changes. Seeing the results in yourself will boost your expectancy and belief in success to the higher level needed to help others.

First, pick three areas of your life that deserve top priority for improvement. I am not telling you which areas to select, but here are some of the common aspects of life that are easily affected by negative and limited thinking, such as a poor self-image. You may decide to pick one or more of these, or entirely different ones:

- Talent (art, music, writing, composing, et cetera)
- Physical skill (typing, swimming, sports, driving, et cetera)
- Health (energy, sleep, allergy, illness, et cetera)
- Wealth (bank balance, investments, possessions, et cetera)
- Social (friends, activities, neighbors, et cetera)
- Romance (marriage, single life, fulfillment, et cetera)
- Business (staff relations, decision making, profits, et cetera)

Once you have selected three areas, whether they are listed here or not, put these three in order of priority and do three exercises, one for each in that order. Here is how. Read these instructions several times until you know them well.

Exercise to Improve a Poor Self-Image

1. Sit in a comfortable chair, close your eyes, take three deep breaths, and visualize some peaceful scenes.

2. "See" yourself as you are now—for example, if you are working on improving health, see yourself listless.

3. Mentally write a big red "CANCEL" over the picture and change it.

4. Now "see" yourself a physical dynamo. You are easily doing whatever needs to be done and then some.

5. Open your eyes, feeling wide awake and dynamic.

Wait an hour or so and repeat this procedure using your second poor self-image aspect. Again, pick a mental image that needs to be canceled and then a mental image the way you would like to be. Wait another hour or so and do the same for the third aspect.

Here are some mental images that exemplify positive self-esteem, at least in a symbolic way. These are just listed to assist you in creating one that best fits your aspirations:

- You are in a theater dressing room with a star on the door

- You are sitting behind a big desk with "President" on it
- You are being carried on the shoulders of your admirers
- You are surrounded by suitors
- You are winning a Mr., Mrs., or Miss America contest
- You are living in a huge house
- You are vacationing in a 5-star hotel
- You are first over the triathlon finish line
- You are the valedictorian of your class
- You are accepting the Nobel Prize

Get the idea? These mental images all have one thing in common—they recognize no limit and program you accordingly.

Why not select a few of these images as applicable to you and, whenever you are alone for a few minutes, use one or two in a daydream to improve your self-image?

Cleaning Up Your Act in Daily Life

In the middle of this century, a Hawaiian man wrote a book in which he divulged many secrets of the Hawaiian kahunas, or wise men. Before the manuscript could be sent to a publisher, a dog got hold of it and chewed it to bits. He rewrote it. While on a voyage aboard the ship on which he worked, a flood once again ruined the manuscript. He wrote it a third time. This time it was published.

What interfered? Coincidence? Accident? Once you understand the nature of higher levels of intelligence and become better aligned with them, you can see that rather than coincidence or accident, there was an intelligent force at work trying to prevent the secrets from being published. Perhaps we were not yet advanced enough in wisdom to use them rightly.

We are now in the age of de-occulting. Ancient secrets are being revealed. Ancient lessons, once incomprehensible, are now better understood. Science is discovering ways to use the brain more efficiently. But this is still a left brain world. The right brain is still little used—like a vestigial organ.

We still worship material ways practically to the exclusion of spiritual guidance. Listen to these words of wisdom from our intellectual giants:

"Energy, like the Biblical grain of the mustard seed, will remove mountains." Hosea Ballou.

"There is no genius in life like the genius of energy and industry." Donald Grant Mitchell.

"The real difference between men is energy. A strong will, a settled purpose, an invincible determination, can accomplish almost anything; and in this lies the distinction between great men and little men." Thomas Fuller.

If you believe your success lies only in the expenditure of energy . . . If you believe that iron-willed determination will get you practically anywhere . . . If you believe that your success lies solely in hard work and sweat—more power to you. But there is an easier way. See you later.

The rest of you, follow me.

You can use all your strength and determination, but it can never equal in accomplishment what you can do with less expenditure of energy when you have help from the other end.

Most American Indian tribes believed in the Great Spirit, which worked through anthropomorphic spiritual personalities with intelligence and emotions and the freedom of will to intervene in the affairs of men. They also believed in an impersonal spiritual power, shared by spiritual personalities, humans, and even inanimate objects. Today we might call these angels.

Just as we who are enlightened know today that the Creator is part of creation, that a higher intelligence permeates all space, so did the American Indian know that his sweat was not the controlling factor in events.

As a result, for example, so successful were the Indians in agricultural activities in those days that the corn and potatoes they originally domesticated now furnish almost half of the food supply of the world.

The American Indian tribes had their medicine men, shamans, and priests, whose specialty it was to intercede for tribal members in order to get spiritual help to solve problems. You are approaching their wisdom and stature, and nobody will have to intercede for you.

Recently, I overheard a man pleading to a minister to help him pray for assistance in overcoming a problem. Replied the minister, "Sorry, I'm not in management; I'm in sales."

To say to the average man in the street today that we are godlike is to invite derision. The same applies to the average man off the street. Two farmers seeing each other at their property edge for the first time in days had this "enlightened" conversation:

"Need rain."

"Sure do."

Period. Not exactly an enlightened conversation.

You have emerged from endarkment by controlled daydreaming. You are on a par with ancient wise men because you have activated your right brain connection to the Creator and all of the angels, fairies, and other extensions of the Creator. You have cleaned up your act in daily living by thinking positively, doing good for others, and reprogramming for more attuned actions and speech.

You are becoming an enlightened person. You have emerged from left-brain, material-world limitations into a bicameral brain existence that combines material and spiritual realms with unlimited possibilities for health, wealth, and happiness.

Eliminating Fears and Phobias that Hold You Back

As an enlightened person, you will enjoy a better and better life. The improvements can come so fast they will take your breath away. Or they can come so slowly as to be almost imperceptible.

Slow progress can be the result of lingering programming of old negative habits, especially those resulting from fears and phobias. Eliminate these dead-weight fears and phobias and you burst ahead.

We are not talking about conditions that cause you to take care and be cautious and concerned. Those are natural. But when conditions are felt as paralyzing, petrifying, or pernicious, they are unnatural. They are the result of experiences that have programmed you with mental blocks that, in effect, block your enlightenment.

Here are a dozen typical everyday experiences. If any are less fun than others to you, or no fun at all, check them for follow-up:

- Flying in a airplane
- Viewing from a high elevation
- Being in a small room
- Speaking in front of people
- Riding in an elevator
- Having a loving relationship
- Seeing an insect
- Taking on responsibility
- Going swimming
- Spending money
- Meeting new people
- Visiting new places

These are just twelve. There are hundreds. If these twelve present no qualms to you, take a moment to reflect on what might give you mental uneasiness. In a moment, we will ask you to pick one latent fear from the above twelve or from your own private collection to represent all of your fears.

What causes are involved in these fears?

There are three major causes:

1. An unhappy event you experienced.

2. An unhappy event you know somebody else experienced.

3. An unhappy event you have been taught may happen to you.

If we look inside our mental "house" for these causes, we probably will not find them because they are "hiding" in the deep subconscious. This might be symbolized by a basement, deep closet, or storeroom. Select such a place in your house or, if it does not exist, imagine that it exists. You are now going to sweep it clean of all causes of fears and phobias that interfere with your optimum behavior, with your connection to the Creator, and with your fullest enjoyment of life.

As you relax and picture yourself sweeping out this place, be sure to notice a piece of litter labeled with the fear you have identified. Read these instructions over several times until you are comfortable with what you are to do:

Exercise to Clear Fears and Phobias

1. Sit in a comfortable chair, close your eyes, take three deep breaths, and visualize a few peaceful scenes.

2. Imagine you are in your basement or a dark closet sweeping it clean of all debris. See this debris labeled with the fear you have just identified. See other debris labeled with fear in general; sweep it all out of the room.

3. When finished, admire your work. How good it feels to be rid of these killjoys!

4. Put your good feelings into words by affirming mentally, "I am now fearing less and less. Every day I have the ability to handle all experiences with more calmness and courage. I have full confidence in myself. And this is so."

5. Open your eyes, wide awake, feeling confident that you fear less.

When ready, put the book down, close your eyes, and program this important step.

Life is now brighter. You have become even more enlightened.

Identifying Personality Weaknesses and Substituting Strengths in Their Place

Just as fears and phobias affect your profit and loss statement, your longevity, and your joy in living, so do some personality quirks and weaknesses. They do arise from past conditioning or programming. They interfere with your enlightenment.

What are personality quirks? Here are some examples of weak personality traits, together with the opposite traits—the stronger traits—for which we might like to exchange them. Just as we listed typical fears, here are ten negative personality traits together with their more desirable opposites:

Weak	*Strong*
Emotional	Phlegmatic
Cries; shows anger, affection, and other emotions too strongly.	Remains calm, stable; more emotionally balanced.
Rigid	Adaptable
Disturbed if routine is upset; prefers own way to others' way.	Flexible to change; able to adjust.
Egotistical	Modest
Takes all the credit; gives others the blame; brags a lot.	Self-effacing; strong self-esteem without flaunting it.
Eccentric	Conventional
Goes own peculiar way in dress, interests, behavior.	Conforms to accepted standards; if original, conservatively so.
Unconscionable	Caring
Unscrupulous; bends the truth; disrespectful of others.	Conscientious about doing what is right and not doing what is wrong.
Hard	Tender
Does what has to be done, regardless of it being upsetting to others.	Sensitive to others; sympathetic and empathetic.
Downer	Upper
Begrudges credit to others; would rather call attention to their shortcomings.	Likes people; knows that by boosting them he boosts himself.

Quitter	Perseverer
Works in fits and starts; slipshod; easily distracted and discouraged.	Strong-willed; sees a job through.
Slow-poke	Go-getter
Lacks vigor; drags feet; vague; undirected.	Forceful; decisive; self-starter; spirited.
Pessimist	Optimist
Sees failure as inevitable; thinks habitually negative thoughts; depressed.	Sees success as inevitable; habitually positive; hopeful.

Pick out those negative personality traits you feel an enlightened person such as yourself should not have. List them on a piece of paper, together with their opposites. Don't limit yourself to the ten examples. Think of others not mentioned that might apply to you. Write them on your list together with an appropriate opposite.

In your next reprogramming session, you will be able to open your eyes and close them quickly again without materially affecting your alpha brain wave frequency. So you do not have to bother to memorize the list of personality strengths you are about to program. Of course, if there are only one or two, you do not need the list, as you can remember them.

Read these instructions several times until you are thoroughly familiar with them:

Exercise to Reprogram Negative Personality Traits

1. Sit in a comfortable chair, close your eyes, take three deep breaths, and visualize some peaceful scenes.

2. Imagine you are at a buffet. You have a plate in your hand, ready to serve yourself.

3. Each choice is clearly labeled with the positive personality strengths on your list. Serve yourself with each, opening your eyes to check the next on your list if you must.

4. Imagine yourself seated, enjoying the meal.

5. Erase the scene and mentally say, "These strengths are now mine. I am more able to perform my creative mission in life. And this is so."

6. Open your eyes, mentally saying, "Wide awake."

Put the book down now and do it.

Before continuing with the next section of this chapter, take a moment to realize what changes you have just made in your approach to living. Daydream about yourself going through a few situations where you react with the personality strengths you have just programmed.

Start thinking about how else you can be improving yourself and becoming more enlightened.

Identifying Destructive Emotions and Programming Productive Ones in Their Place

Emotions are important. They are the batteries that trigger our behavior. Without emotions, we are powerless. With emotion, we have the power to act.

You are not about to make yourself free of emotions. That is absurd. But you are about to help yourself in a way worth thousands of dollars to you. You are about to soft-pedal destructive emotions that, like personality quirks, get in your way of being a truly enlightened soul and closer to the Creator.

Destructive emotions, like unwanted personality quirks, can be derived from past experiences, or they can be a result of present conflicts or troubles.

Here are some examples of personal questions from the past as well as in the present that might point the finger at their origins:

Early Childhood

Were you an only child?

Were you disciplined physically or by the threat of it?

Were you sexually abused?

Were you spoiled by your parents?

Did you feel you were an unwanted child?

Adolescence

Were you disciplined as much as when a child?

Did you feign illness to get what you wanted?

Were your parents constantly arguing?

Were your parents constantly voicing disappointment in you?

Was your home atmosphere unpleasant?

Present Time

Are there major differences between you and your mate?

Are your children a source of worry to you?

Is there a third party threatening your marriage?

Do you or your spouse have physical difficulties that are bothering you?

Have there been any deaths in the family?

~George wanted to be happy, but he kept experiencing problems that kept him pessimistic and in a state of near depression. He began to feel happiness would never be his lot. He was attracted to a four-day mind training course. He was not happy when he started. He was not particularly optimistic about a possible improvement. But by the middle of the second day, he was surprised and delighted with his progress. He began to feel a rapport with the other students. By the end of the third day, he noticed that his emotions were reversed. He was looking forward to each step in the training. And when the four-day training was complete, he felt he was walking on air. He could not think of anything to be unhappy about or pessimistic about.

"I realized who I am," he said. "I am an
important part of something much bigger."

You are quite likely a bigger and more important person
than you think yourself to be. Destructive emotions are holding you back. You have no need to regress in time to identify
dark causes of dark emotions. It is not in such darkness that
the answer lies, but in the light. Identifying the problem always helps in programming a solution. Pause a moment and
see if you can put your finger on one or more of your destructive emotions and their causes.

You are now going to create an additional room in your
house. It will never need cleaning because it is the source of
cleanliness and purity itself. When you are in this room mentally, you will be able to expunge all destructiveness from your
emotions and substitute brilliance and creativity.

This room will be an addition to your home or apartment.
You will create four walls, a floor, and a ceiling. You will furnish and decorate the room any way you wish as long as the
walls are white and the colors bright. The walls will be the
source of light. You will have a chair and a desk and on the
arms of your chair will be a dial you can use to turn up the
light to greater brilliance. This will be a cool light. Instead of
heat, it will have love. The more light, the more love.

Here are the instructions for adding strength and creativity
to your emotions. Read them over carefully. There are two
parts to the session. Here are the instructions for the first part.
For simplicity's sake, when you have completed the first part,
we will give you instructions for the second part. To begin the
instructions for the first part, read the previous paragraph

about the room and its furnishings until you are confident you know what to do.

Now put the book down and begin.

Exercise for Adding Strong and Creative Emotions

1. Sit comfortably in a chair, close your eyes, take three deep breaths, and visualize a few peaceful scenes.

2. Create the room as described above.

3. Open your eyes, affirming mentally, "Wide awake."

You are now ready to begin the second step in this upgrading of your emotions. Read over these instructions several times until you are sure what to do:

1. Sit in the chair and turn the control in the arm of the chair, which brightens the light.

2. Enjoy the brilliant white light that fills the room. Feel the love that this light contains. Know that you are part of this light. Know that all is well.

3. Mentally affirm, "I erase the negative legacy of the past and react with positive feelings at all times."

If you have the instructions down pat, put the book down and do it.

You are becoming a more limitless person. Starting immediately, you will notice that people admire you more. You are being recognized as an enlightened one.

～

5

The Trick of Consciousness that Gives You a Breakthrough to Joy

⁓from Quajagan, Sufi master

The attainment of joy is the thrust of this chapter. Probably the most skillful people on the matter of joy were the Sufis, especially the whirling dervishes.

The Sufis were Moslems that had mystic practices. They were located mostly in Persia in the eighth century A.D. Some were known as whirling dervishes because they practiced whirling dances accompanied by the chanting of spiritual affirmations in order to achieve a collective ecstasy.

By the eleventh century, the Sufis were inspiring a new poetry that used magnificent imagery to proclaim the love of God. The Sufis, including

Quajagan, who was a Sufi master, sparked a shift in emphasis from the concept of divine transcendence, or that which is beyond the limits of human understanding, toward the concept of divine imminence, or that which is existent or inherent now. It brought God closer to humankind and their belief system.

Quajagan was not as well known as some of his peers. Al-Ghazzali, a professor at a theological school in the twelfth century, was influential in the founding, endowing, and supervising of many such schools that produced an increasing number of Sufi saints. These saints were known for their mystical contemplations and wise utterances intended to arouse similar mystic feelings among their listeners.

We have much to learn from ancient cultures in the search for a better life. You might say that, because of the advanced civilization in which we now find ourselves, the material world has more than ever before throttled our connection to the Creator.

You are now involved in the most powerful self-help program available to humankind. It not only brings about fortuitous happenings and enables you to cope with challenging situations, it also bestows gifts such as better sex, new culinary experiences, peace of mind, peaks of joy, and unexpected gifts of appreciation from others. I know. I've been there.

It is not an exaggeration to call the contents of this book the most powerful of self-help programs, because the help comes from the most powerful force in the universe, the very Creator.

The Sufis knew that the greatest source of knowledge comes from deep intuition. What is deep intuition? It is the voice from within, the connection to the Creator. I am not your teacher. Your teacher is the Creator.

The Culprit that Acts to Block Your Joy

When you begin to open the door to unbelievable joy in your life, you know where it comes from. There is no greater source of power, no greater source of knowledge, no greater source of joy.

There is a factor in your life that sneaks up on you and does its dirty work. It not only blocks your joy in life, it drains your energy, blocks your enlightenment, erodes your vital organs, and ultimately can kill you.

That culprit is stress.

When you recognize stress and learn to control it, as you will now, all the factors in your life that we have been reprogramming take a quantum leap forward. You are more positive and optimistic. Your personality improves. Family and friends relate better to you. Your joy begins to manifest more fully. Life changes for the better.

Stress does not announce itself. When you are under intense or prolonged stress, no bell rings, no warning siren goes off. Instead, your nerves feel frazzled; your blood pressure rises; you become "impossible" to others; your immune system protects you less; vital organs begin to malfunction. So it is essential that you recognize stressful conditions promptly and take evasive action.

The threat of stress is around you constantly. Some jobs are continuously stressful, such as law enforcement, flight control, and handling complaints. Other jobs become stressful only when the chips are down, such as staff reduction, sales contests, and depressed businesses. People in the following jobs are also potential targets for stress: miners, stockbrokers, medical interns, waitresses, and secretaries.

Stress comes in your personal life at such times as during marital difficulty; getting a traffic citation; losing a close friend or relative by death; having a fire; being robbed or trespassed upon; having an accident. Most people do nothing about it and prefer to wait out the mental discomfort. They are inviting progressive trouble: a mental state of helplessness; the advent of mental depression; depletion of brain chemicals; weakness of the immune system; physical illness. Sometimes a single event can cause continuing stress. Continuing stress can be a killer.

For instance, if you are attacked at night, days later the event is fresh in your memory and still a cause of stress. You remember it. You relive it. You go over again and again in your mind what you should have done but did not do and what you did do that you should not have done. As you remember the event and relive its horror, your body reacts as if it is happening again.

If your home was ransacked or you caught your spouse being unfaithful or discovered that your partner was stealing from you, the stress at the time of the event may be gone the next day, or the next, or the next, and then maybe not.

Life produces multiple events, many of which are stressing. So you may be under a bombardment of stress.

Both parents are under stress when a child is unmanageable or a teenager goes astray. Staying within a budget can be stressful when it becomes obvious that you are not succeeding and the bills are piling up. Your neighbor's dog can cause you stress when it barks at night or defiles your garden; here again, your neighbor's not seeing eye to eye with you about the problem only magnifies the stress.

The telephone or the television set can become an instrument of stress if it entails competition among family members. The weather can be stressful when it upsets routine with extremes of snow, wind, or rain.

The Good Side to Stress

In prehistoric times, when man was a hunter, he was often confronted with a ferocious wild animal. Immediately his body responded. His body hair stood on end to make him look larger—we still feel this happening when we are faced with an eerie condition. His heart beat faster and harder. His breathing quickened. Acid was released in his stomach, which in turn stimulated the glands needed for fight or flight.

These were lifesaving reactions to stress for him. Besides the hair standing on end, we still produce acid in our stomach but, because there is no way to fight or flee from modern-day stress, the acid remains and, with the help of eagerly awaiting viruses, causes ulcers and other conditions.

Stress was helpful to ancient man and is still helpful today under certain conditions, like when we are about to be tested in some way that involves optimum skill and ability. Stress helps in an emergency where quick thinking and action is needed. Stress helps when you are appearing before an audience to talk or perform. Stress helps the athlete to compete more effectively.

How to Be Less Affected When Stress Strikes

You have already acquired "first aid" against stress.

By thinking positively and helping others dispel the crush of stressful events on you, you are blunting the mind-piercing aspects of stress. By closing your eyes, taking three deep breaths, and visualizing peaceful scenes, you are taking the sting out of stress. By putting your two fingers together, you are reinforcing your connection to the greatest antidote against stress—the Creator. By making positive affirmations, you disarm stress. In fact, if the situation does not permit you to sit comfortably, close your eyes, and take three deep breaths, you can make certain mental affirmations that can be quite effective in protecting you. Here are some examples:

This too shall pass.

So what?

God is with me.

Everything happens for the best.

Let go and let God.

Things get better and better.

This will be a perfect day.

Here are some of the body's warning signs that stress is beginning to seriously affect you:

- Intestinal distress
- Rapid pulse
- Insomnia
- Persistent fatigue
- Nail biting
- Irritability
- Memory lapse
- Nervous tics
- Lack of concentration
- Hunger for sweets
- Increased use of alcohol
- Resorting to drugs
- Frequent illness

If you are a business person, add absenteeism to the above list. And give it a special name: Burnout!

Some of the things you should do as part of daily living in order to lessen these effects of stress are:

- Maintain a sense of humor—let the joke be on you
- Seek to be alone more in order to relax
- Exercise more: walk instead of ride, take the stairs instead of the elevator

- Get a massage, buy a new shirt or hat, go to a humorous play or movie

- Eat more sensibly and limit your intake of alcohol and caffeine

- Delegate responsibility; stand up to the boss, even quit

These are "first aid" measures. When you are home and have time to yourself, you can take more effective measures against stress, measures that afford real and permanent protection.

The first and most basic protection is extended periods of deep relaxation. Refer to Chapter 2 for ways to deepen relaxation. Then, while in a deep state of relaxation, pick one peaceful scene and stay with it. Preferably select a place you have been that is associated with nature, like a beach, a meadow, a mountain, a lake, a stream, et cetera. Do this for about five minutes two or three times a day.

What to Do If Stress Leads to Depression

Depression can be an outcome of stress. It is tantamount to a death wish. When you are depressed, your will to live is throttled and aging is accelerated. Your family will know that you are in a depression, but tell them just in case. It is not a state that you should try to sweep under the table. Now it is not a matter of having a better life. It has become a matter of having a life at all. Your family may insist on your seeing a therapist. That may be a good idea.

Meanwhile, besides doing the longer periods of relaxation already described, use the other aids elaborated on in this chapter.

This may sound superficial, but it has had a profound effect on some people's depression: Dispel gloom with light. Here are some of the ways:

- Use white dishes and china
- Wear white or brightly colored clothing day and night
- Keep the rooms you occupy as brightly lit as possible with natural light, with venetian blinds open and shades up
- In the evening, turn on a few extra lights
- If optically safe, avoid the use of sunglasses

If I were to advise you to think positively when possible, this would be impractical advice. A state of depression, by definition, is one where positive thinking is practically impossible. However, it is possible to reprogram your mental computer in a positive direction. This is done by relaxing and giving yourself positive affirmations to repeat. We will now supply some recommended affirmations. Why not enlist the help of a friend or relative to read these important instructions to you while you are relaxed?

If you are in a depression now, include these affirmations, read to you by a second person in your periods of relaxation. Use only one at a time, but have it repeated several times.

Start with this. Mentally repeat the words as they are read to you.

**I feel down. I want to feel up. When I open my eyes,
all negativity will have left me and all worry
will have vanished. When I open my eyes,
any darkness will have left me
and the world will look much brighter.
Eyes open.
Wide awake to a brighter world.**

Repeat several times each day for several days before switching to this next one.

**I am becoming calmer, stronger, and more secure.
Every day, in every way, I become more interested in life,
optimistic, and enthusiastic. I am more and more in control,
happier, and more confident.**

Again, repeat several times each day for several days. Then, with eyes open, have this third affirmation read to you and see how it feels. If you think you are ready, conclude your period of affirmations with this final one. Have it read to you several times a day for several days.

**I am a creative person. I get ideas. I solve problems.
Higher intelligence assists me with answers and solutions.
I make progress whether I see it or not.
My expectations are high.**

Congratulations. You have been uplifted.

Goal: To Rise To a Higher Level of Consciousness

They say that one of the surest signs that intelligent life exists in outer space is that none of it has tried to contact us. We certainly have a long way to go if we are to behave in ways worthy of spiritual beings. Some ancient cultures appear from the present point of view to have been ahead of us. The inspired souls of the past who are helping me with this manual are examples of being connected meaningfully to higher consciousness.

The ultimate objective of the Sufis was perfection of the individual and union with God. Some of the noblest and most spiritual characters in Islam emerged from Sufism. Their unceasing awareness was to surrender to the will of God.

The Dervish were a mystical fraternity within Sufism. They were headed by a sheik who became their leader by dint of his esoteric knowledge. Such knowledge had no earthly sources at that time in history and could only come from deep intuitive reception. Part of this knowledge was an understanding of the importance of joy. So it was that the Dervish embraced singing and dancing in the spirit of fun and acquired the name Whirling Dervishes. Often, to outsiders, they appeared to be in hypnotic or ecstatic states. What was being observed, however, were undoubtedly those peaks of joy that can only be properly described as celestial.

Every chapter in this book so far has been devoted to helping you rise to a higher state of consciousness. Since this means become closer to being godlike, the steps have included ways to become closer to the Creator. Becoming closer to the Creator is not to say you are becoming more religious. Some may say you are becoming less religious. What you are becoming is more a part of the larger intelligence—the higher consciousness—that fills all space. This chapter is no exception. It, too, will give you what you might call a trick to elevate your consciousness to a level that may make you gasp.

To succeed toward this end, I helped you handle the stress of this material world. Stress can be strong enough to be a dead weight on consciousness, preventing growth and spiritual advancement. As you are now aware of how to recognize stress and how to defuse it, you are closer to being able to seek the joy in life that comes with a higher consciousness. One more step that is preventive of backsliding is needed. You must remember to program out any negative emotion as soon as you recognize it and to program an opposite emotion in its place.

Closing the Door to Backsliding

Listed below are the "most wanted" negative acquisitions— that is, most wanted for elimination. Alongside each are the opposite mental attitudes that need to be reprogrammed into your mental computer to take their place. These are the ten most common sets. You can undoubtedly add to the list.

Program Out	Program In
Worrier	Confident
Easily upset	Resilient
Weak	Strong
Overwrought	Tranquil

Driven	Purposeful
Gloomy	Cheerful
Competitive	Cooperative
Critical	Appreciative
Aloof	Outgoing
Impatient	Patient

You can program out any one of these unwanted aspects of yourself that can be a drag on your progress toward enlightenment, joy, and a great new life. All you need to do is enjoy a one-minute relaxation and controlled daydreaming session once a day for three days.

If you are host to more than one of these anchors that are holding you back, use the next three days to program another one out and its opposite in. And so on. Here is how.

Read these instructions over several times until you are sure of how to proceed ("worrier" has been used as an example):

Exercise to Reprogram Unwanted Personality Traits

1. Sit in a comfortable chair, close your eyes, take three deep breaths, and visualize some peaceful scenes.

2. Repeat mentally, "I am frequently a worrier. I no longer wish to be a worrier. I wish always to be confident. Every day I am becoming more and more confident."

3. See yourself worrying; then visualize a big "X" over this mental picture.

continued

4. See yourself assured and confident.

5. Open your eyes, wide awake, feeling confident.

Now put the book down and do it. Repeat two more days.

Expanding Your Consciousness for Greater Joy

Now that we have neutralized the inhibitors of joy, including tendencies to backslide, we are ready to move ahead.

Greater joy in life is possible only with a greater capacity for joy. This requires a rise in consciousness. Tricking your consciousness can produce such a rise. Before we utilize this trick, however, your consciousness will respond more fully if we begin now by raising it in a more standard way.

When you read the next three true accounts of what exists, their unbelievable aspects, in order to be accepted by you, require your consciousness to be elevated. So, sit back comfortably as you read and prepare to be bewildered, if not stunned, but certainly expanded.

Migrating birds are extraordinary. Some have powers that far exceed any known in humans. Some see ultraviolet light, even polarized light, as well as they see standard colors. Flying thousands of miles, they return year after year to the same tree, even the same branch. The plover flies from Hawaii to northern Alaska in spring to mate. In late summer, it returns to Hawaii, with the baby plovers following in about six weeks. Yes, they are helped by the stars. Some even sense the Earth's magnetic field. But stop and think whether you could even come close to doing this yourself.

Now, conceive of what plants can do. Cleve Backster, one of the foremost polygraph experts in the world, has been able to electronically monitor plants and human body cells and detect reactions, both positive and negative, to human thoughts and actions.

It all started when he was cleaning up after teaching a class in the operation of the lie-detector equipment to New York City policemen. He decided, on the spur of the moment, to monitor his house plant to see how long it took for water to go from the pot to the leaves, using the lie detector or polygraph.

He attached the electrodes to the leaves, turned on the read-out, and decided to go get water. Instantly there was a positive spike in the read-out. He wondered about that, but then went and got the water, and poured it. Instantly, there was another positive jump in the read-out marker. The plant reacted positively! That floored him. Could the plant read his thoughts?

He decided to get a match and burn a leaf. Instantly, before he could act on this thought, there was a negative read-out on the chart. There was no doubt communication was going on. The plants appeared to "know" his thoughts.

Hundreds of experiments followed. Plants reacted to his killing shrimp in boiling water, swatting a spider, even men's urine hitting an antiseptic urinal in the nearby men's room.

He set the read-out going on a plant when he left for a walk. When he decided to turn around to come back, he looked at his watch. When he got back, there was a spike on the chart at that exact time. When he repeated this, but decided ahead at what time he would turn around, there was no reaction at that time. The plants already knew.

An example of this primary perception in human cells appeared on television's *Incredible Sunday.* A woman's mouth cells were taken, placed in solution, the electrodes inserted in the solution, and the read-out turned on. The chart showed a mildly wavering straight line. Meanwhile, the woman was taken to a run-down neighborhood where she was dropped off and kept in the sights of a hidden television camera. Viewers could see a split screen picture of both the read-out chart and the woman as she walked amidst beggars and homeless people. Suddenly, she was confronted by a huge bearded man. Instantly her cells, three miles away, reacted. There was a strong negative spike in the otherwise gently wavering line.

I visited Backster's lab and had my mouth cells similarly extracted and electronically monitored. As I looked at the beaker several feet away, I sent love to my mouth cells. Instantly there was a sharp positive spike on the read-out chart. I then reached for a breath sweetener. Instantly there was a sharp negative spike as my mouth cells reacted to the use of this strong chemical on their brethren still in my mouth.

Your body cells know your thoughts! Sit on that one for a while.

Now for that trick in consciousness that expands that consciousness and opens you to incredible joy.

Remove This Barrier and Let In a Flood of Joy

In the famous Sermon on the Mount, Jesus said:

> And when thou prayest, thou shalt not be as the hypocrites are: for they love to pray standing in the synagogues and in the corners of the streets, that they

> may be seen of men. Verily I say unto you, they have their reward. But thou, when thou prayest, enter into thy closet, and when thou has shut the door, pray to thy Father which is in secret; and thy Father which seeth in secret shall reward thee openly.

What you are about to do is like a prayer and so must be done in secret. That is, the people involved should not be told about it and the action itself should be done in a place where solitude for a few minutes is guaranteed.

What you are about to do is become an emotional alchemist. You are going to change your hate of certain people into love for them.

Hate, mistrust, jealousy, animosity, and any other negatively polarized feeling you may have against somebody is, like stress, a ballast that keeps you from rising as you deserve to new heights of abundance, energy, and joy.

Think of three people that have crossed you up so badly in the past or present that just mentioning their name makes your blood curdle. Examples might be the person who seduced your mate; the policeman who gave you a speeding ticket; the business partner who dealt behind your back; the family member who did you wrong; the person who took credit for what you accomplished; the gunman who held you up. You don't have to know their location, and distance is not a factor.

We say three people—there may be fewer but more likely there are more—because three are the most that it would be advisable to process at one sitting. You may continue later to identify more for additional work.

But it is really not work.

~Betsy had an instructor in her community college who called her in because of her poor grades. What became obvious in the consultation was that he wanted sexual favors in return for passing grades. She refused. He did not give up. Each time he scheduled a private meeting with her, he became more and more forward. When he began groping and fondling, she complained to the department head. Nothing happened. She flunked the course and was lacking credits to graduate.

It was only after three years working as a sales person in a department store that the college recognized sexual harassment and established corrective procedures. Betsy was sure then that this instructor would now put his hands in the wrong place and get his due punishment. However, she knew his wife and children, and the more she thought about it, the more pity she felt—not only for them but for him, too, acting the way he did out of quiet desperation.

Betsy relaxed and pictured him. She forgave him for being so forward. She imagined a handshake as sealing the mutual bargain of forgiveness.

She had forgotten about this a month later when a large envelope arrived from the college. It was her diploma. A letter from the dean, enclosed with it, explained that an error had been discovered by that instructor and she had really passed the course. Her newly acquired diploma led to a better job and unbounded joy. She no longer hated the instructor. She felt love.

Hate cannot become love directly. To be a successful alchemist in transforming hate to love, you must go through forgiveness first.

If you had to go to your mother-in-law's house, ring the bell, and stand face to face with her in order to forgive her and ask to be forgiven by her, you would probably dismiss the whole idea from your immediate plans and it would never really happen. Thanks to a trick of consciousness, you do not have to go through such a painful routine. You can sit in your living room, close your eyes, relax, and visualize the whole mutual forgiveness procedure. It then becomes real. Your mother-in-law may phone you and say how much she really appreciates you, or in some way confirm that your feeling good now about her has become a two-way street.

Forgive me for involving your mother-in-law as an example, but that relationship is traditionally a stressful one. Select three of the people most unworthy of forgiveness, and you will be choosing the ones you need most to forgive.

"I'll never forgive that s.o.b.!" declared one of the men at my all-day seminar on metaphysics.

"You are only hurting yourself, not him," I reminded him. "Pretend he is a child who was brought up that way and did not know any better. Surely, a child deserves to be forgiven." The man agreed, forgave the ex-s.o.b., and felt better for it.

Have you picked three? We will call them A, B, and C. Let's go. Read these instructions over until you know well what to do.

Exercise to Forgive Others

1. Sit in a comfortable chair, close your eyes, take three deep breaths, and visualize a single peaceful scene.

2. Returning from the peaceful scene, invite A into your room.

3. Standing in front of A in your mind's eye, forgive A and ask to be forgiven. "See" a hug or a handshake.

4. A leaves. Invite B. Repeat.

5. B leaves. Invite C. Repeat. C leaves.

6. Open your eyes, wide awake, loving all three.

Put the book down and do it now.

How is it possible for a feeling such as forgiveness to be transmitted any distance? This is one "trick" that will be explained, contrary to the magician's code.

Actually, it is not a trick. It is a feature of the non-material world.

The forgiveness goes to your higher self and then to the other person's higher self, as the two higher selves are connected via the oneness of all in the Creator. Yes, we are all connected in a spaceless, timeless realm where we all came from.

To know so is to expand your consciousness. To do so is to know a quantum leap in joy.

As Consciousness Expands, Joy Rises, and Beliefs Become Less Limited

I would like to tell you three stories. They appear to be unrelated, but they do have a common denominator. See if you can put your finger on it after you have read the stories.

Story number one. It is during World War II. A famous liner, the Queen Mary, is making its first voyage across the Atlantic as a troop carrier, ferrying American GIs to Great Britain. The waters are submarine infected, so the ship is blacked out at night.

Six WAACs—Women's Auxiliary Army Corp members—are bedding down in hammocks for their first night at sea in a cabin meant in peace time for three. For hours they toss and turn in the stuffy cabin, unable to sleep. Finally, one of the women gets out of her hammock and goes to the porthole.

"I know we are not supposed to," she announces to the others, "but I am going to open the porthole; nobody light a match or a flashlight."

"Yes, do it," the others urge.

When she cranks open the porthole, they all breathe a sigh of relief and sleep like babies that night. In the morning, when they go to close the porthole, they see it is sealed with an outer glass pane and no fresh air had entered the cabin through it that night.

Story number two. A woman is walking her four-year-old along a sidewalk in a suburban area where they live. The child runs on ahead. Suddenly, a Cadillac parked in a driveway begins to roll slowly backward. It pins the child under a wheel.

The mother dashes forward, lifts the Cadillac's wheel, and the child is freed. The mother weighs about 100 pounds, the Cadillac over 2,000 pounds. Similar events have happened again and again, always baffling those involved.

Story number three. A person suffers from an allergy called rose fever. This allergy causes the person to suffer a pesky cough, watering eyes, and a stuffed nose every time there are roses nearby. This person with rose fever walks into a room where there are imitation roses made of plastic. Immediately this person gets all the symptoms of rose fever.

There you have it. Three stories: The porthole that never yielded fresh air; the rescue of a youngster from under a Cadillac's wheel; and the allergy symptoms that appear with plastic flowers. What one word describes the cause behind all three stories?

Did I hear "belief"? Correct.

Belief in an open porthole was as good as having it opened. Belief in saving the child was incentive for the strength to do it. Belief in there being real roses convinced the body it was time to start the symptoms.

Your beliefs about yourself affect your behavior. If you have conscientiously followed the instructions in these five chapters, your beliefs about yourself have been radically changed. You realize that your consciousness has been expanded. You know that, as a result of this, you are now a more capable person. Part of this revised belief system involves the understanding that you are closer to the Creator.

Does this mean that, if you are treated unfairly, you can give the working out of a situation over to the Creator? It does.

Does this mean that, if you are faced with great odds, the Creator will provide you with the courage and strength to prevail? It does.

Does this mean that, when you find yourself on a dead-end street with no place to turn, the Creator will open up a way for you? It does.

Does this knowledge bring you joy?

Joy unbounded.

Is this deserving of a word of thanks to the Chinese seer, the Druid priest, the Greek naturalist, the American sachem, and the Sufi master who, among others, guided the author over the years and through the writing of the first half of this manual for a better life? Indeed it is.

Let the thanks be through your higher self to whoever it belongs. Read these instructions over until you know them well. Then put the book down and do it. Here is how:

Exercise to Give Thanks

1. Sit in a comfortable chair, close your eyes, take three deep breaths, and visualize a favorite peaceful scene.

2. Invite your higher self into the room. You mentally see your higher self arrive—tall, radiant.

3. Mentally rise and hug your higher self, saying "I love you."

continued

4. Mentally add, "I am closer to the Creator now and will need you more than ever."

5. Your higher self gives you a "yes" in any of many ways—a smile, a nod, a verbal assurance. Your higher self leaves.

6. Reseated, you open your eyes, feeling wide awake and rejoicing in your advancement.

Because of the progressive steps you have taken in these five chapters, you can now create with your imaging power specific benefits, such as money, love, health, and more. Besides your obvious visible means of support, you now have an invisible means of support.

You may dance with joy. But it is not necessary to go so far as to become a Whirling Dervish!

~

6

Daydreaming Your Way to Unlimited Wealth

~from Huktutu, Mongolian shaman

*T*he Mongolians of Northern Asia were a people with mysterious powers, invested mostly in their shamans, or priests. The shamans were believed to be able to summon spirits to help them do their will. They also had mediumistic powers. They used visualization to create.

It seems miraculous that nomadic tribes, such as those united by Ghengis Khan in the twelfth century and later mixed with Turkish nomads under Batu, could conquer vast lands south to China, southwest to Turkestan, Iraq, and Iran, and northwest into Russia.

They were called the Golden Horde. Although they amassed wealth with their conquest, their cities prospered as cosmopolitan trading centers along routes the Mongols secured across Asia. The culture they instilled raised the standard of living. They were in power in China at the time of Marco Polo, who was astonished at the affluence of their royal court. But eventually, their basking in luxury led them to ignore the need to stay armed to protect themselves and they were overpowered.

Our source in this chapter is more modern than most others. He is a Mongolian shaman named Dilawa Huktutu. He was the last living Buddha of Inner and Outer Mongolia before the Communists took over in the middle of this century.

As a monk, he was detached from seeking wealth yet, despite this, abundance followed him—he never wanted for anything and his needs were miraculously met. Disciples felt overwhelmed in his presence by his loving compassion. When the Communists overran his country, he escaped to the United States, where he lived until his death in the 1960s. (Recently, we learned from a traveling Mongolian dance troupe that the Dalai Lama had confirmed that a fourteen-year-old boy in New Jersey was the reincarnation of the holy man Huktutu.)

Would you like to prosper like the Golden Horde? This chapter will show you the way. But it assumes that you have solidified your connection with your higher self and the Creator pursuant to the procedures in the previous five chapters. Even so, you have work to do before you can manifest cold cash.

Just as there are obstructions to your being a channel for the Creator, there are obstructions within you specifically damming up the flow of money. Remove these by following the instructions on the pages ahead and watch out for a blizzard of dollar bills!

Negative Programming that Costs You Money

Poverty is a state of mind, as we will now demonstrate and help you to alleviate. It is why the rich get richer and the poor get poorer.

There are many ways that it is possible for you to mentally reject prosperity. First, we will put the finger on beliefs you may have accepted—and this means programmed—in your early years. Here are some examples:

If your parents were poor, you were constantly barraged by the apparently inescapable fate that you, too, would be poor. According to a psychological study, when a person makes a negative statement to you as a child, it takes nine positive statements to undo the damage by the one negative statement.

If you had a low self-image, no matter how rich or poor your parents, you were constantly programming your mental computer that you are not capable of earning a lot of money and so you will never be wealthy.

If you were not necessarily poor yourself, but you knew a number of poor people, you saw how they never materially improved their status, thus programming yourself that once poor you stay poor.

Religious beliefs can, through the years, program you with some wrong beliefs about money. "Money is evil" is a common religious belief. "Only crooks have money" somehow managed to survive to this day as a precept of wealth with no basis in truth. "Money is dirty" is another.

These religious beliefs may have started centuries ago through a misunderstanding of Jesus' Sermon on the Mount. For instance, Jesus is quoted as saying:

> No man can serve two masters; or either he will hate the one, and love the other; or else he will hold to the one and despise the other. Ye cannot serve God and Mammon.

In the same Sermon are the words:

> Lay not up for yourselves treasures upon earth, where moth and rust doth corrupt, and where thieves break through and steal; but lay up for yourselves treasures in heaven, where neither moth nor rust doth corrupt, and where thieves do not break through nor steal; for where your treasure is, there will your heart be also.

It is to those who abandoned spiritual concerns in order to live a material life that Jesus was aiming these words. Money was necessary in those days to survive, as it is now. And later, the Church itself had to preach about the importance of money to exist.

Up until this day you have been exposed to a speech mannerism that kept you in a state of consciousness not conducive to the flow of wealth you deserve. Money does not grow on trees. Nobody is going to do for you what one woman did for her husband's birthday to get him to change his mind about that. She got up early and pinned dollar bills to leaves outside his breakfast window.

A penny saved is a penny earned. That one is attributed to Ben Franklin. It would have been better had he said, "A thousand dollars saved is a thousand dollars earned." The resulting effect on people's minds would have been more rewarding.

Other beliefs that you need to flush down the drain are instilled by statements like, "Money goes out a lot faster than it comes in." "Artists must struggle" (or actors, writers, et cetera). "I treat everybody first, then myself." "I don't deserve . . . ."

Author Louise L. Hay, vital proponent of prosperity, tells of the student who came to her class all excited because he had just won $500. "I don't believe it," he kept saying, "I never win anything." He obviously felt he did not deserve it. The following week he was absent from class because he had broken his leg. The doctor bills were $500.

Nobody likes to take the blame for their own poverty. But it is one's beliefs about wealth or poverty that dictate one's lot. You must decide to change your consciousness about wealth if you are to manifest it.

Simple Changes in Thinking that Let the Money In

It makes you no richer if you boost your own self-image when actually that is not one of your weaknesses and you really think quite highly of what you have done and what you can do.

You have to analyze your beliefs and pinpoint those particular beliefs that are negative, limiting, and act as a put-down to money or material possessions.

How do you feel if somebody says to you, "This is a universe of abundance. So claim your share." Do you feel angry at them? Or disbelieving? Or think that the statement is a lot of wishful thinking?

How do you feel about spending money? I don't mean that you should be like the woman who, when criticized by her husband for overspending, replied, "Name one other extravagance." I mean, do you feel guilty?

How do you feel when you see a pile of bills on your desk waiting to be paid? Do you see them as an enemy trying to conquer you? Or, perhaps, as a depressing fact of life?

These are the kinds of attitudes that make the poor stay poor and perhaps get even poorer. Think like the wealthy instead of like the poor and you begin to let the money in.

Yes, this is an abundant universe and the money is trying to come in, especially if you have grown in consciousness over the past five chapters.

You can sit in a comfortable chair, close your eyes, visualize a favorite peaceful scene, and then substitute a positive way of thinking for a negative one. Mentally say, "I no longer (this). Instead I (that)."

Then, reinforce this programming from time to time, both mentally and physically; mentally by repeating the relaxation and affirmation, physically by some action that demonstrates the positive thought. Some of these actions may seem distant to you now. But after programming, you will understand them better.

These actions might include:

- Treating somebody to a soda or a meal
- Paying a bill that is not due yet
- Tipping somebody extravagantly if they deserve it
- Buying yourself a new tie or hat
- Sending something to a good cause
- Saying something nice about somebody's financial luck

If you cannot do these things without feeling some remorse, you are still blocking universal abundance. Have a talk with yourself. By that I mean for you to relax and make positive affirmations.

Here are some.

How to Talk Yourself Wealthy

While relaxed, with your eyes closed, repeat one of these affirmations—the one that you feel you would resist the least—several times a day for several days:

> **The words I now mentally repeat bring health, happiness and prosperity to me. I offer myself to the Creator as a productive channel.**

> **I dedicate myself to manifesting the abundant life as a direct result of my devotion to the Creator.**

> **I am all-wise, all-powerful, all-conquering because infinite wisdom guides me and divine love prospers me.**

Why not start now? As soon as you have selected one of these three affirmations, memorize it, relax, and repeat it mentally three times. Do it now.

Anytime you make a change for the better in your life, the universe applauds. You begin to have coincidences, synchronicities, and little "miracles." These are caused by the Creator. A coincidence is an event designed by the Creator but not signed. You begin to have spiritual experiences that you can neither describe nor explain.

Somebody said, "If you have your head in the stars and your feet on the ground, you better pull yourself together." I disagree. You are already "pulled together." You have a connection to the Creator. You bring the resulting insights back into how you live your life.

⟿ Mental programming is bringing new wealth to
people every day. Take Jean. At 23, he became
proprietor of an inn, but lost it. Intuitively he knew
that he should not let this financial blow affect his
thinking. He relaxed and gave himself positive
affirmations.
   Then he read *The Silva Mind Control Method
for Business Managers*[1] written by me together with
Jose Silva, founder of that mind training course.
He got a marketing manager's position and,
using the mental tips provided in the book,
built winning sales teams.

Louise L. Hay, authority on prosperity quoted earlier in this chapter, writes that she blesses and loves each bill that arrives in the mail, and kisses each check she writes to pay it. She blesses her telephone each time she uses it, affirming that it brings her only prosperity and love. She does the same with her mailbox and her front door.

Can you imagine yourself doing this? And, if you can, can you also imagine the positive energy that would surround your abode, attracting a flow of abundance to you?

---

1. Silva, Jose and Robert B. Stone. Englewood Cliffs, New Jersey:
   Prentice-Hall, 1986.

What Life Energy Has to Do with Your Bank Account

There is an energy field that surrounds the human body. It is the blueprint for the physical body, the pattern that sets the structure upon which the cells of the body grow. This energy field can be measured and, for what is especially important to you, it can be altered.

In order to appreciate the importance of this field, you need to know that it is not only the vehicle for the mind/body connection that affects your health (see Chapter 8), but it is in touch with other energy fields that affect your family, your circumstances, and your relationship with the other side. In fact, what happens to you takes place in these energy fields first.

Let us hold a mirror up to you at this very moment. Is there something that is happening or has happened where you feel you did not do the right thing or where you could have done something better? Or is there something about yourself that you cannot fully accept? Everybody has some aspect of themselves that they deplore. What they don't realize is that such an attitude affects their energy field. It creates a distortion that acts as an obstruction to the flow of energy and to all that depends on that flow of energy—health, relationships, flow of wealth, and well-being.

A research scientist at NASA's Goddard Space Flight Center, Barbara Brennan, has studied and measured the human energy field for twenty years. She believes that when you have something within yourself that you won't accept, "You actually create distortions in your own energy pattern that have to do with unforgiveness towards yourself." She further states, "When you forgive yourself, you are actually unblocking the flow of energy in your field so that it can flush itself out. It allows for the resumption of the normal life flow."

We don't care who you are or what you do, you need to forgive yourself. Despite your military medals, your prize-winning accomplishments, and your adoring family, you will benefit by forgiving yourself.

In fact, it needs to be such a thorough job that we will divide your self into three parts so that you can forgive each part separately. The three parts are your subconscious, your conscious, and your superconscious.

Here are three experiences that will cleanse your energy field for a greater flow of all that is good—including, of course, money.

Improving Your Status with the Most Important Person in Your Life

You will now forgive yourself, starting from the bottom up—the bottom being the deepest aspect of your mind, the subconscious.

The subconscious is like a subterranean chamber where all memories are stored. You can bet your bottom dollar that these memories include many that are holding you back and holding back the flow of the energy of wealth.

At separate sessions, each taking only a minute or so, you will then forgive yourself at the conscious and superconscious levels.

Carl Jung noted that the mind symbolizes its own deep aspects with bodies of water. We will now use that symbol to gain the end so valuable to you. You will see your reflection in the water and forgive that reflection; here is how.

Read these instructions several times until you are sure you know exactly what to do.

Exercise to Forgive Your Subconscious

1. Sit in a comfortable chair, close your eyes, take three deep breaths, and visualize your favorite peaceful scene.

2. Imagine you are walking through a peaceful valley, then a forest of giant strength-inspiring trees, and you enter a clearing where there is a placid pond.

3. Stand at the edge of the pond and look down at your reflection in the still water.

4. Repeat mentally, "I forgive you for all past failings and misunderstandings and ask that you forgive me." Then add, "I love you."

5. Mentally return the way you came.

6. Open your eyes, wide awake.

You may now put the book down and do it.

The most important person in your life has three parts. That person is you, but don't look to see if your body is in three parts, because you are not your body. You are your consciousness, which is your "handle" on life. It is your consciousness that is divided in three parts.

You have cleared the air with one part—your subconscious. Now comes your conscious. That leaves your superconscious. It is preferable that you follow up each as soon as possible. Are you ready to take the second step now? Then here is how to forgive your conscious mind.

Read these instructions several times until you are sure you know exactly what to do.

Exercise to Forgive Your Conscious

1. Sit in a comfortable chair, close your eyes, take three deep breaths, and visualize your favorite peaceful scene.

2. Imagine you are standing in front of a full-length mirror. You can see yourself from head to toe.

3. You don't like what you see. All of your past mistakes and shortcomings are labeled on your image. You draw a big X over your reflection. You mentally say, "I forgive you."

4. You imagine you are turning full circle to the right and are once again facing your full reflection. This time it is your perfect self. Mentally say, "Forgive me." Add, "I love you."

5. Open your eyes, wide awake.

Put the book down now and do it.

The final step is simple. It involves your higher self. You have greeted your higher self before. You are familiar with the procedure. But here are the instructions. Read them carefully so that you know them before you begin.

Exercise to Forgive Your Superconscious

1. Sit in a comfortable chair, close your eyes, take three deep breaths, and visualize your favorite peaceful scene.

2. Imagine that a person has entered the room. Mentally "see" this person to be you, but taller and bathed in radiant light.

3. Mentally rise, face your higher self, and say, "Please forgive me for all past mistakes and misconceptions." Pause and add, "May this forgiveness be mutual."

4. Mentally embrace your higher self, saying, "I love you."

5. Mentally return to your seat and open your eyes, wide awake.

Put the book down now and do it.

You will feel an elation at reaching this point in attaining a richer life. This is due to an increase in the flow of life energy. Your energy field has been cleared of blockages that prevent its flow between you and your body cells, between you and other people, and between you and other forms of energy, such as money.

Expect better times.

Striking While the Iron Is Hot

If you have a serious need of money, now is the time to use your imaging power to create it.

It is only human to do something that you are not totally satisfied with in the days ahead. This will besmudge your energy field. Even if it is a mild altercation with a fellow worker, or a neighbor, or a family member, it will have a money-preventive effect on your energy field.

Right now that field is in perfect order, ready to react to your creative imagination.

Do one of the following exercises only if you have a valid and urgent need for a sizable amount of money. We say only one exercise, because if you do more than one, it is because you don't expect one to work. This lack of belief is a no-no. You're right. It won't work.

Priscilla did the Ball of Light exercise and came into $75,000. Ashton got an unexpected tax refund. I received a royalty many times what I expected.

The Universal Bank exercise is not used universally. It appears to be more popular in the western part of the United States. The Money Angel exercise requires a more critical need than the other two.

Choose one. Read the instructions only for the one you choose, otherwise your choice may be based on factors related to the instructions rather than your need. Know the instructions for the one you choose well before you start.

Ball of Light Exercise

1. Take a denomination of money and keep it handy. The larger the denomination, the bigger the return.

2. Sit in a comfortable chair, close your eyes, take three deep breaths, then place the money on your lap.

3. Imagine a large ball of light about a foot over your head. It is the size of a basketball.

4. Mentally move the ball of light slowly down, encompassing your head, now inside your body, letting it move slowly down until it reaches the level of your navel.

5. Imagine a beam of light emanating from the ball of light and shining through your solar plexus (just above the navel) onto the money on your lap.

6. See the money getting charged with energy from the light.

7. Mentally withdraw the beam of light.

8. Mentally send the money out into space.

9. Mentally see a million bills of money in all denominations flying back at you. It is like a money blizzard.

10. Move the ball of light slowly up to the position above your head where it started and let it disappear.

11. Open your eyes, wide awake.

In the next twenty-four hours, rid yourself of the money on your lap, either by spending it or changing it.

If you know all the steps, put the book down and do it now.

Universal Bank Exercise

1. Sit in a comfortable chair, close your eyes, take three deep breaths, and imagine a large city. There is a stately columned building in front of you. Above the columns you mentally see the words "Universal Bank."

2. Go up the few stone steps and enter the bank through one of the main doors, then go over to the table where there is a supply of blank checks.

3. Mentally write a check payable to yourself for an amount dictated by your need, not greed.

4. Mentally walk over to a cashier and hand in the check. See the cashier nod smilingly, indicating approval.

5. Mentally leave the way you came.

6. Open your eyes, wide awake, knowing the solution to your financial need is on the way.

If you know all the steps, put the book down and do it now.

Money Angel Exercise

1. Sit in a comfortable chair, close your eyes, and take three deep breaths.

2. Invite your higher self into the room; when this larger version of yourself appears in your imagination, mentally embrace and say, "I love you."

3. Ask your higher self to please call your guardian angel into the room.

4. When you imagine your guardian angel entering the room, say, "Thank you for all your past help."

5. Next, mentally explain to your guardian angel how much money you need and the reasons you need it.

6. Mentally thank your guardian angel and your higher self and open your eyes, wide awake.

If you know all the steps, put the book down and do it now.

Idiosyncrasies to Avoid in Handling Money

Once money arrives to pay your bills or to permit some venture, you are not necessarily out of the woods.

Psychiatrists and psychologists have identified several idiosyncrasies and neurotic attitudes that people frequently have about money. These can be pitfalls that bring you back to where you started. Before we go into them, it is important that you realize for money to continue to flow into you, it must also flow out. Yes, you can save some and indeed you should, but remember that the Creator's wealth must be kept flowing. You are a channel for this wealth and to be able to enjoy it on a continuing basis, the channel must not get blocked.

Now for the peculiarity in money habits to watch out for.

Some people have no focus or goals when it comes to money. So they are likely to spend it thoughtlessly. Many go on shopping sprees as a way of boosting their self-esteem. This may have sounded like you before starting this book, but with the reprogramming you have been doing, it's probably just a memory. At any rate, check your spending. If you are using your credit cards with abandon, give yourself this reprogramming:

I love the Creator for the bounty supplied me;
I use it wisely, honoring the Creator, every time.

By relaxing and repeating this affirmation several times a day for several days, you will probably find that you have cut up all but one or two of your credit cards, and have increased your savings allotment. You will find you are going into stores less frequently and buying only what you need.

Some people use money for the excitement of gambling. They bet money on the horses, on the blackjack table or on the stock market. If they win, they feel good, if they lose, they keep gambling in order to recapture that good feeling.

If you are a gambler, you are probably addicted as a source of excitement. Just as we can become addicted to sex as excitement, we can become compulsive about gambling. So I am not going to ask you to program yourself not to gamble. Rather I am asking you to change races—from horses to humans. Betting on the human race can be even more exciting. So can changing games, as from poker or dice to the game of life.

This is the affirmation, repeated several times a day for a few days, that will turn the trick:

> **I love the Creator for the bounty before me.**
> **Every day, in every way, what comes to me**
> **I use creatively and constructively,**
> **gambling it in the game of life.**

Then there are people who are compulsive savers. This may not lead to the recurring shortages experienced by spendthrifts or gamblers, but it can work against one's prosperity, too.

If life's abundance is blocked because of some dead-end street, it seeks another path. We attract wealth because we are channels for that wealth. Specifically—creative channels, and paths of fun. Benjamin Franklin, to whom is attributed "A penny saved is a penny earned," also said, "The use of money is all the advantage there is in having it."

If you are not spending some of the incoming flow on having fun and fulfilling your dreams and aspirations, you are, in effect, a dam to the natural flow of life energy as represented by the money. You are creating less than you can.

If you are cramping your style and that of your family by stashing your money where it is safe from being spent, you are probably up to here in fear of a rainy day. If so, reprogram yourself with the confidence-building affirmations in previous chapters. Or use the following one:

> **I love the Creator for the bounty before me.**
> **I seek a balance between using it for good now**
> **and using it for good later.**
> **I conscientiously fill my assigned role as a co-creator.**

Used several times a day while relaxed in the usual way, this reprogramming will enable you, contrary to the way the saying goes, to have your cake and eat it, too.

Other Forms of Wealth that Are On the Way to You

That last affirmation is of universal benefit, for spenders and non-spenders alike. Filling your role as a co-creator is the common denominator for wealth. And it comes in many forms.

⁓John was a chronic baseball fan. He not only went to every home game in Cincinnati, but traveled to other cities. When he told his boss at the brokerage where he worked that he had to go to an aunt's funeral, his boss shook his head, not only in compassionate grief but in astonishment that so many aunts could be lost in so brief a time.

John was at a standstill in the company. His clients were, too. His boss would give him some ideas from time to time, such as encouraging him to look into the latest Internet developments or aerospace companies. John accepted the advice enthusiastically, but followed up instead on the day's major league scores.

One day, when John announced the "death" of another member of his family, his boss hit him squarely in the eyes with, "You've got an addiction to funerals, John." He handed him a slip of paper. "I recommend you see this psychologist." John took his advice.

The psychologist used hypnotism and gave John anti-baseball suggestions that took root. But, to his credit, the psychologist also gave John some positive suggestions to fill the gap left by baseball, such as: You will enjoy your brokerage work more and more as you use your financial knowledge and intuition to greater and greater advantage for yourself and others.

As John's attendance improved, so did his devotion to creative investing. He and his clients prospered as never before, and so did his marital relations. In fact, he and his wife found a new mutually enjoyable hobby—sailing on a nearby lake. But not during office hours.

Wealth comes in many forms, when its time has come. Yours is now. The Creator is crediting you.

Again quoting Ben Franklin:

> The longer I live, the more convincing proofs I see of this truth, that God governs in the affairs of man; and if a sparrow cannot fall to the ground without his notice, is it probable that an empire can rise without his aid?

A Daydream that Pays Off Handsomely

Each of the three exercises to create quick cash given earlier in this chapter—Ball of Light, Universal Bank, and Money Angel—involved visualization and daydreaming. That is because a creative act was involved and imagery is directly involved in the creative process. The processes given you to neutralize idiosyncrasies in the handling of money included no imaging, only reprogramming with affirmations. That is because what was being accomplished was not creating, but changing behavior.

It is always productive to daydream creatively. It would now be productive to daydream that your quick cash has arrived and you are using it to fulfill your needs. Here is how:

Exercise to Reinforce Money Exercises

1. Sit in a comfortable chair, close your eyes, take three deep breaths, and visualize yourself at the usual place you handle money matters at home or at work.

2. Mentally see yourself preparing a deposit. You are elated and full of energy. Hold this moment in your mind for a few seconds, letting it play itself.

3. Mentally repeat, "I love the Creator for the bounty before me and conscientiously fill my assigned role as a co-creator."

4. Open your eyes, wide awake.

Read these instructions several times and memorize the final affirmation. Put the book down and begin.

Whenever I teach these methods for obtaining wealth to an all-day class, I always conclude with, "Don't forget my ten percent." Of course, it is meant as a joke and indeed it always gets a laugh. They do not owe me ten percent and neither do you.

I might go so far as to say you even do not have to tithe with this money, that is, you are not obliged to give ten percent to a house of worship. The reason is you have already pledged to use it for the Creator's work. Do what you wish to do, but . . . all earned wealth belongs to the Creator. We all work for the Creator to help make this a better world to live in.

~

7

Daydreaming Your Way to Unlimited Love

~*from Iriana, sorceress of the Berbers*

"I love humanity. It's people I hate." Whoever said this certainly did so in jest. But, unfortunately, it is quite common.

To some, "love" is a dirty word. Because they think so, it is.

To others, "love" is something you may feel but find too dangerous to express. So you don't.

"Love is what makes the world go around." This saying comes closest to the truth. Without love in the universe, there would be no law of attraction, no gravitational pulls, no solar systems, no galaxies. Probably no sex, either.

This chapter helps you to attract more love in your life. It is not limited to using your relaxed imaging power, but this daydreaming is certainly a vital part. It goes beyond daydreaming to some physical and metaphysical approaches to obtaining relationships—from sexual to soulful.

Throughout the chapter, one truth prevails that will be repeated from time to time. It is universally true but universally difficult to apply. Here it is: You receive as much love as you give. No matter which of the remarkable steps you take to manifest more love in your life, as spelled out on the pages ahead, you will receive only as much love as you give. Period.

So the first step we need to take has apparently nothing to do with receiving love—only with giving it.

Some Secret Reasons Why You Find It Difficult to Express Your Love

The more love you express in your daily life, the more lovable you yourself become. Priority number one: "How do I express more love in my daily life?"

Love is natural. So to answer the question of expressing it more, we need to find out what is blocking it. Once we identify the blocks, we can program them out, and reprogram a loving nature in.

To know more about such blocks, we have guidance from the distant past. Iriana, sorceress of the Berbers, comes through with a surprise. She repeats the word "Aloha." This is a Hawaiian word for "love." What has it to do with the Berbers, who were a Northern African Caucasian people?

Research turns up little hard information. The Berbers valued their freedom and eluded control by others even though they lived in communities from Egypt to the Atlantic Coast and from the Sahara Desert to the Mediterranean Sea. Originally, they had their own language, but apparently were so considerate of others that they spoke the language of any country they were in.

They were creative with pottery, weaving, and embroidery. The men were largely farmers. All were poets and usually put their poetry to music. The Berbers were apparently so appreciative of other peoples that they were frequently absorbed by them, especially by the Arabs.

Then research hit the jackpot: A visitor to North Africa several decades ago met a Berber who still knew the ancient Berber language. This visitor was part Hawaiian and, to his amazement, the Berber language was chock full of similarities to the Hawaiian language!

Any connection to Hawaii is a connection to love. You cannot say "hello" or "good-bye" in Hawaiian without saying "I love you," as the word "Aloha" means all three. So, if you were brought up as a Hawaiian, you would have no problems with expressing love.

But, you were not. So you do.

You are created by a Creator and therefore are born a reflected image of the same. But, in a few years, you become a reflection of your parents and others who surround you. When you berate others later, you are doing what your parents did to you as a child. You might even use the same words.

You spilled your milk. "Clumsy!" You walked on a newly planted garden. "Stupid!" You break a toy. "Crazy!"

You acquire a self-image of being clumsy, stupid, and crazy. You get even with others by bringing them down to your level, shouting what epithets? Clumsy, stupid, and crazy. You might still be doing it. If your parents never praised you, not only do you not feel praise for yourself but neither do you feel praise for others.

However, do not blame your parents as they were acting the way they learned from their parents, and so on. It is now up to you to break the cycle. It is an important cycle to break because it interferes with receiving love in your life. You are probably acting in a way that causes a fellow worker to be irritable, your boss to be unappreciative, and others to turn their back on you.

Is that what you want? Of course not.

A Daydream that Programs Daily Love

The first we hear of the Berbers is their arrival in Egypt about 1300 B.C. from other parts of North Africa. They came in search of food. By 200 B.C. they had settled south of the Sahara and were skilled iron workers. Soon they became a vital part of the whole North African scene, dominating the Mediterranean coastland.

They became famous far beyond their own lands for the beauty and speed of their horses. But they contributed very little to matters of historical value. Could this be the result of their friendliness and loving nature rather than a warlike nature? Even today, journalists and historians tend to dramatize wars and ignore the quiet waters of serenity.

Eventually Berber cities acquired Roman habits and customs and many Berbers became citizens of Rome. Today, there are about fifteen million Berbers with a variety of Berber dialects. They are almost all Moslems and follow Arabic traditions and customs.

My mental impression of the Berber source known as Iriana is one of overwhelming love. Perhaps love is an area you would like to change in your own life. To begin to change, you need to want to change. You need to want more love in your life and be willing to give more love in your life to others.

Think of one, two, or three people who do not treat you the way you would like to be treated. We will call them A, B, and C. You will use these people in the exercise that you are about to do that will reprogram your own behavior.

Read over the following instructions several times until you are convinced you know the steps you are to follow:

Exercise to Express More Love

1. Sit in a comfortable chair, close your eyes, take a deep breath, and visualize a favorite peaceful scene.

2. Imagine the first person, A, the way you usually see him or her—at work, at home, et cetera. Feel a lack of rapport.

3. Mentally say, "I want this to change in the direction of a greater expression of love."

4. Mentally forgive this person. Imagine an immediate change for the better.

continued

5. Do the same with B and then with C.

6. Repeat mentally three times, "I am more and more understanding and loving every day."

7. Open your eyes, wide awake, knowing that a more loving world awaits you.

When you know this procedure, put the book down and do it. Repeat three times a day for three days.

Do you demand immediate results? Will you blow up if your boss gives you a hard time tomorrow? That would not be loving, would it?

Understand that you are changed and, as you express this change—be it with patience, jocularity, or courtesy—your change will cause others to change. It is well worth waiting for.

But you do not have long to wait.

Transform Physical Love from Cool to Hot

When Clarence was a boy, his parents never kissed in front of him. When he saw a couple doing so on a park bench, he asked his mother what was happening. The answer: A tug on the arm and an "Oh, never mind."

His room was next to his parents' room and, by the time he was ten, he began to notice that on Saturday nights they locked the door and he could hear them pull down the shades. Then there was a bouncing of the bed springs. In a few minutes, it stopped, and then he heard their toilet flushing.

Clarence talked about this with his peers. He found out that his parents were having sex—not making love, but having sex. When his own maturity arrived and relationships with girls began, they were fleeting. He wondered why, even by the age of twenty-five, he had not developed a single lasting relationship.

Soon Clarence met a young lady who insisted on remaining a virgin until she married. So he married her. Within a year they were at a marriage counselor. There this whole story unfolded. It was a familiar one to the counselor, who gave Clarence and his bride some required X-rated reading. This changed Clarence's way of looking at himself as a male stud. He became instead a loving male mate.

If you have a disinclination to show affection with your family or with people to whom you are attracted, it is probably not for the same reasons that tripped up Clarence. But, whatever the reasons, such coldness on your part induces equal coldness on the part of others.

Here is how to warm up the situation: Write your own X-rated movie. Daydream about Marilyn Monroe, if you will, ravishing you with hugs, kisses, and affection and you, as her leading man, reacting to this ecstasy. I am not going to have anything to do with this movie. It's your party. You are the author, the director, and the lead.

See this movie in the privacy of your own daydream. By this time you know how. Read these instructions several times:

Exercise for Sexual Love

1. Sit in a comfortable chair, close your eyes, take three deep breaths, and visualize a movie screen.

2. Mentally see your X-rated movie. Run it as long as you wish.

3. Open your eyes, wide awake, realizing it could be a true story. Repeat as needed.

Put the book down and do it.

A coolness toward demonstrations of affection may be connected with religious training that taught sex was dirty. If expressing love and tenderness causes you to fear that it might lead to the sexual act, you would avoid such expressions. You don't want to dirty yourself.

This avoidance spreads to include all people. Don't look now, but you have become a cold fish. Affection is an important aspect of love where individuals are involved socially. It is not a turnpike to sex. You can put your arm around somebody, male or female, and your action does not have to be misunderstood. If you love a person, showing affection is natural. Affection later becoming more intimate in sex is natural.

Furthermore, sex is not dirty. Sex is the ultimate expression of love and love is the ultimate expression of spirituality. Is spirituality dirty?

My words on these pages blaring forth as trumpets will not change you. You must want to change and you must reprogram in order to change. The following reprogramming procedure is recommended when a relationship is being interfered with by a partner's belief that sex is dirty.

Read these instructions over several times until you are thoroughly familiar with them.

Exercise to Dispel the Image of Sex as Dirty

1. Sit in a comfortable chair, close your eyes, take three deep breaths, and visualize your loved one naked.

2. There is a sliding glass door between the two of you and it is so dirty that you can hardly see through it. The naked body is partially obscured by the dirt.

3. Mentally affirm, "I want this to change."

4. Imagine your partner stepping forward with a rag and cleaning the glass door.

5. You can now see the naked body clearly and it is beautiful to you.

6. Open your eyes, wide awake, noting your changed attitude toward sex.

If you know the procedure, put the book down and do it now.

Drawing People to Your Side

Before you can love humanity, you must love people. Before you love people, you must be able to love a person. Before you love a person, you must be able to draw such a person to your side to better know them.

"Know" is not used here in the carnal sense, but in the broader person-to-person sense. Before you can love a person, you must know their assets and their shortcomings, their beliefs and disbeliefs, their likes and dislikes.

This cannot be done at a distance. So how do you draw a person to your side? If you are cold, unfriendly, and aloof, you are repelling rather than attracting. Should this describe you, all is not lost. There are ancient rites that still work today; we understand them, not as some magical power, but as a tool to help change their user.

An example could be the placebo. If a doctor does not know how to cure you, he might prescribe a sugar pill. You do not know it is a sugar pill. You think it is some powerful medicine with the "magic" power to cure. You take it as prescribed, and you are cured.

Ignore what I have just told you. Consider the few steps about to be described not as placebos but as powerful charms and incantations. Know that they work. They may not have started with the Berbers, but they were used by them and other ancient peoples.

~Stephen and Lucille were to be married. But she met somebody else who, she said, needed her more. Stephen, crushed in spirit and wallowing in despair, decided to use his knowledge of metaphysics to win her back from Chicago, where she had gone with this other man.

Lucille had left her equestrian gear with Stephen, her riding habit and boots. Stephen sat in a

comfortable chair with this gear on his lap. He
closed his eyes, took three deep breaths, and
pictured the gear as Lucille herself. As he caressed
them, he imagined her feeling his love. Mentally he
asked, "Would it not be good for you and for me to
be together?" When he opened his eyes, wide
awake, the work was not finished. He took the
clothes into his car when he went to work; he
placed them in his bed when he went to sleep.
In a few months, Lucille called from Chicago.
Would he meet her at the airport? In two weeks,
they were married.

All the instructions you need are in this story. If you choose
to do it, be sure it is the person you want to be closer to, because it works.

Another way to draw a person to your side, to know them
better, involves simple visualization while relaxed. Mentally
"see" the person standing in front of you. Whisper into the
person's left ear (on your right, if the image is facing you). Tell
the person that you would like to explore a possible friendship
or love affair. End your relaxation on a note of expectancy.

How to Use Body Language
to Attract Others

Do you know that you are in possession of one of the most
powerful tools to attract other people? That tool is silence.

When used in the proper place at the proper time, silence
can be irresistible. Silence reflects super self-confidence. I took
a class in government at MIT when I was enrolled there. It was

a small class of about ten students that met informally around a table with the professor and chatted. I never opened my mouth for the four-month semester. Yet I received an H (Honor)—the highest mark. Obviously, the professor was impressed with my silence.

Here is how silence can be combined with body language to radiate irresistible self-confidence:

- A man leans against a wall, his thumbs hooked under his belt, fingers pointing down

- A girl, seated, leans nonchalantly on her elbow, swinging her crossed leg

- A man looks upward thoughtfully, ignoring everyone around him

- A girl stands next to a person she would like to know better, taking no part in the group's conversation, and leans toward that person just enough to touch shoulders

The eyes have traditionally played an important part in bringing people together. Psychologists have discovered that when a person sees something he or she likes, there is an expansion of the eye's pupil. Contrarily, when a person sees something unlikeable, the pupil of the eye contracts.

This helps to explain why, in all cultures, large expressive eyes are considered an asset. You have been noticing this yourself. When people's eyes "light up," you know they are glad to see you. When people are angry, their eyes become like narrow slits.

Over there is a person you would like to know better. Do you greet that person with your eyes in narrow slits? Of course not. You would not get very far. Instead, you open the aperture of your eyes slightly. You do not stare, but you hold eye contact a bit longer with eyes open a bit wider. Now this could be a good time to express your wish vocally. Maybe, "Do you have time for a cup of coffee?"

In a few minutes you will likely be asking, "Cream or sugar?"

The Importance of Self-Confidence in Attracting Love

Usually people look for inspiration in other people.

Yes, writers are curious about other writers. Artists are interested in how other artists get their inspiration. Businessmen hope to get inside information or new approaches from other businessmen. Fundamentally a person is interested in how another person lives their life in the hopes that they can benefit by doing something similar in their life.

The basic attraction is success.

Are you attracted to a person out of work? Or a person shabbily dressed? Or a parent with an offspring in prison? These types seem to be losers. What do you have to gain in fanning such a friendship? So, you pass. But, when you come across a person who exudes self-confidence, your reaction is positive.

Now put yourself in the other person's shoes. To attract that person, you must reflect confidence. How do you reflect confidence when there have been a number of shortcomings in your talents or behavior to date? The answer is: Reprogram.

What is it that undermines your self-confidence? Do you set unreasonable standards for yourself? Do you have a fear of intimacy? Were you in love once and hurt by it? Do you have feelings of unworthiness? Are you stung by criticism? Perhaps a parental relationship has given you a feeling of being unlovable.

You don't necessarily have to identify the cause of your feelings of being unworthy of love. We will provide new programming that will overwhelm the old and give you the new—the new being self-confidence that radiates irresistible attraction.

If you are able to identify the cause, insert the second step of these instructions. Read this several times until you are totally familiar with the steps, including the words of the final affirmation.

Exercise to Build Self-Confidence

1. Sit in a comfortable chair, close your eyes, take three deep breaths, and visualize your favorite peaceful scene.

2. If your confidence has been undermined by a specific person and/or event, mentally picture those details as if they were happening at the moment. Then mentally draw a big red "no" over the picture.

3. Now "see" yourself surrounded by an admiring throng. Each person is anxious to attract your attention.

4. Mentally repeat three times, "I love myself and I am loved by others. I am free of all limiting past experiences. I attract only loving people into my daily life. And this is so."

Then put the book down and do it.

How to Attract a Certain Special Person

Love is the greatest power in the universe. It can drive men and women to commit atrocious crimes. Or it can lift them to the highest peaks of ecstasy. To be without a lover or loved one is to be empty. To be without the person you long for is to be driven to desperation.

We have reached a point in this chapter where we are going to confront the issue of lovelessness head-on. We are going to assume that there is a person you long for and things are not working out.

This is an age-old problem. It was faced by many cultures and tested by many occult practices, going back even before the Berbers to days of King Solomon.

The Hebrew Kabbala, or Science of the Prophets, is a book containing ancient mysteries known only to the Jewish rabbis of old. These wise men wanted these secrets preserved for the future, but not in such a way as to help anyone undeserving. So the Kabbala was written quite esoterically and, even today, the average person sees it as a collection of riddles.

You now know how creative mental images can be. The ancients often recorded their successful mental images, whether

Figure I: Solomon's Seal

based on reality or symbolism. Solomon's Seal (Figure I) is
such a record. Today these ancient diagrams still perform faith-
fully. They create for you in ways that defy explanation.

Solomon's Seal has the power to bring two people together.
Are you yearning to be with a certain person? Would you like
to see this person drawn to your side as if by some unseen
power? Solomon's Seal will help to do it, if no person will be
hurt by it—such as that person's mate, if that person is married.

But there is a price to pay. Free will still dominates the actions of those involved. You must be willing for that person to

leave if such is his or her will. Agreed? Then, here is how. Read these instructions over now, then again after you have traced the Seal and have the picture, until you are convinced that you know the steps and the words of the affirmation.

Exercise to Draw a Loved One to You

1. Trace Figure I, Solomon's Seal, onto a piece of paper. If love or physical attraction is your motive for wanting the person to come to your side, use a red crayon or red felt pen to trace with. If you can find a luminescent red, even better. It will add light and power to the procedure.

2. Obtain a photo of the person you wish to attract, or make a sketch that represents the person to you.

3. With the seal tracing and photo or sketch on your lap, sit in a comfortable chair, close your eyes, take three deep breaths, and visualize the person.

4. Feel great respect for the seal. Then place the seal face to face with the photo or sketch.

5. Mentally say, "If it is the Creator's will, so be it."

6. Open your eyes, wide awake.

7. Keep the seal and photo or sketch with you wherever you go, still face to face, keeping it if you drive in your car, and in the office, or at work, and under your pillow at night, until you meet.

Put the book down and get busy!

The Importance of
Impersonal Love

Love is universal. It is rampant around planet Earth particularly.

Say the Swedish: A life without love is like a year without summer.

Say the Spanish: Man, woman, and love originated fire.

Say the Argentines: The one who loves you will make you weep.

Say the Hindi in Asia: Since love departs at dawn, create, O God, a night that has no morn.

Ram Dass puts it well when he says, "You are no longer a Buddhist or a Hindu or a Christian or a Jew or a Moslem. You are love, you are truth. And love and truth have no form."

We have been covering the subject of love from the point of view of special friends and romantic relationships. But to truly have a better life, you have to understand more about love than the limited approach so far in this chapter.

It is difficult to love the people of your town. You know so few of them and you know so little about those whom you do know. How about loving the people in the next town? Well, you might say, that's carrying love a little too far.

Is it really? Think about this: All humankind shares a common intelligence besides their own private intelligence. As mentioned earlier, it is what Rupert Sheldrake calls the morphogenetic field of intelligence and which Carl Jung identified a century earlier as the collective unconscious. It might even be admitted by scientists a century from now that an intelligence fills all space and may well be what we call the Creator.

Can you love somebody whom you do not know in person, but who shares the same intelligence with you? How can you not?

This is being realized more and more, not by nations necessarily, but by individuals here and there. These are individuals who already enjoy the better life that you are working toward with the use of this book. They have it because of that realization—that we all share the same intelligence.

They are able to love humanity because of the realization of its oneness. And they have a faint inkling that evolution is moving us all into one living organism that will save the planet from the destruction toward which it is now heading because of a collective self-awareness.

Abraham Maslow, the father of humanistic psychology, reports that people are acquiring a profound sense of what he calls "unitive consciousness." Once the domain of only yogis and mystics, this higher state of consciousness has been found to be at the alpha level. The alpha level is the brain frequency you have been experiencing when you sit in a comfortable chair, close your eyes, take three deep breaths, and begin to "see" with the mind's eye.

You have been developing a higher state of consciousness. *Quid erat demonstramus.* The whole purpose of relaxing and imaging is to activate the right brain hemisphere, as you recall, which connects us to the creative realm and, of course, to the Creator. You cannot get much higher in consciousness than that.

You have actually been rising in consciousness to a point above the average human on earth. As you live your life with this greater perspective, people who oppose you, criticize you, or do you wrong no longer appear as monsters with evil thought, but as children with undeveloped thought.

And—can you not love a child?

Your Wavelength and Your Purpose in Life

If you have been following the chapter-by-chapter program in this book—that is, putting the book down and doing the exercises, you are probably beginning to feel that you are on a different wavelength than before. Encourage that feeling in yourself. It's a promising one. It promises more help from the angels, more attention to you from the other side, more love from the Creator.

Let that feeling translate into more love from you. With your life moving to a higher level of joy, you can afford to let go of the barriers you have been erecting against love.

The best is yet to come. Before you finish the last chapter, I am confident that you will reach a state of consciousness where you will begin to lose all sense of separateness and move toward a feeling of oneness with all.

That is the ultimate state of love.

You will be the same person. Your family will see you as the same person. You can walk along with a sidewalk crowd and you won't stand out in any way. Still, there will be two essential changes that are non-physical. You will be more loving. You will better understand your purpose in life.

This may mean nothing important to your lawyer, your accountant, your banker, or your business associates. They will hardly notice any change, except they may listen to you more closely, take you more seriously, and appreciate the wisdom of your advice and decisions on matters with which they are concerned.

This may mean nothing dramatically important to your family either. Nobody will be keeping score; but if they were, your parents and you may be on the same side of an issue more frequently. Your children will be pestering you more fastidiously but you will enjoy it. Your mate will be happier in bed.

You are finished with the kinds of disruptions that life dealt you before. Blockage, repression, and hostility should now lead to smoother sailing, greater self-certainty, and downright imperturbability.

The two essential changes that bring this on, as mentioned before, are being more loving and knowing your purpose in life. Usually the first leads to the second. But, if this has not been the case for you, here is a two-minute exercise that encourages this understanding of one's mission. Read these instructions over several times until you are thoroughly familiar with the steps.

Exercise to Know Your Purpose

1. Sit in a comfortable chair, close your eyes, take three deep breaths, and visualize your favorite peaceful scene.

2. The scene disappears and in its place is your higher self, taller than you and bathed in brilliant white light.

continued

3. Rise, embrace your higher self, and be seated.

4. Mentally ask, "What is my mission in this life?"

5. Your higher self steps aside and points to a mental screen in that standing place. Your higher self leaves.

6. Repeat the question mentally and watch the screen expectantly. A picture of you in some activity associated with your mission or destiny should appear. Let it play itself out.

7. Open your eyes, wide awake, and think about what you just mentally observed.

Put the book down and do it.

A Buddhist Meditation Practice that Builds Love

Once you are convinced about what your mission is, you will find yourself maneuvering to gradually be there, if you are not already on that path.

You will get unbelievable help in the process. There will be coincidences and synchronicities. There will be accidental meetings and lucky happenings, events that will help you get on the right track but will have nothing to do with accident, luck, or coincidence. You will become comfortable with the idea that the Creator and the angels are working with you and you will recognize divine guidance in even the most gentle whisper.

There is a Buddhist meditative practice that is quite powerful. The Sanskrit word for love is "Metta." If you sit in a comfortable chair, close your eyes, take three deep breaths, and mentally repeat the word "Metta," it gives your consciousness a love boost.

You could add other positive love-related words such as, "May I be filled with love and understanding." Or, "May I become more and more loving every day." Always end by again repeating, "Metta, Metta, Metta."

We don't have to go back in time in order to find affirmations that are powerful and effective. You are now able to put together your own words that act to inspire your consciousness to new heights of divine wisdom.

**I am in tune with divine wisdom
even in the midst of my activities.**

What's wrong with that? Or . . .

**Creative energy is in every cell of my body and mind
and is one with the Creator's wish for me.**

Not bad, eh? What about . . .

**Thank you, my Creator, for your love
that flows through me now.**

Got the picture? You're on your own.

∼

8

What's Wrong with Your Life and How to Fix It

~from Bessie of Pulangan, Baltic seeress and healer

*J*f you have been putting people up instead of down . . .

If you have been going out of your way to help others . . .

If you have been instructing yourself while relaxed to have positive attitudes and constructive behavior . . .

If you are becoming less of a pessimist and more of an optimist . . .

If you have been recognizing and neutralizing stress . . .

If you have been replacing hate with love through forgiveness . . .

If you have exalted your belief about yourself through loving your higher self and the Creator . . .

If you have reprogrammed limiting beliefs about wealth . . .

If you have programmed an abundant life . . .

If you have forgiven and affirmed your love for yourself . . .

If you have performed a metaphysical exercise to solve a cash shortage . . .

If you have removed blocks to your expressing love, personal and impersonal . . .

If you have programmed body language to attract . . .

If you have attracted that special person, if one exists, to your side . . .

If you have permitted yourself to rise in consciousness . . .

Then there should not be anything wrong in your life to fix, except one major department—which we will divulge in a minute. But don't think you have gone the distance.

What the Human Mind Is Capable Of

This book falls far short of taking you through the whole route of human capability. If it did, here are some of the things that would become commonplace for you.

- You could mentally leave your body and go through walls and over vast distances

- You could have a profound effect on other people without leaving your home or office

- You could move forward and backward in time

- You could enter the consciousness of another person to know his or her thoughts
- You could heal yourself and others even at a distance

The only single thing that remains is something that no book can help you attain but which is the one spiritual accomplishment that can create the greatest miracles in your life: Overcoming the apparent separateness between you and the rest of the world; that is, uniting with the universe and thus attaining cosmic attunement.

So, you see, you may have come a long way in a short time, but you cannot possibly have gone as far as you can go.

Therefore, things in your life are not yet perfect. It is best to maintain your desire, expectation, and belief that your life will move closer to abundance, joy, and success. Anything negative in your mind can abort those dramatic changes already underway but not yet manifest.

Your Health as a Measure of the Good Life

Help for this chapter is coming from the other side through a relative of my wife's who was on this planet two centuries ago, Bessie, a seeress and healer who lived in the town of Pulangin, in the small country on the Baltic Sea still known as Latvia.

The people of Latvia, called the Letts, evolved from several ancient Baltic tribes of the thirteenth to sixteenth centuries, a period dominated there by the Teutonic Knights. Strength and valiance bolstered by buoyant good health prevailed to such an extent that their exuberance broke into song. Rich folk music was performed by choirs developing by the 1800s into great national song festivals.

We think you will agree that Bessie has given us, in this chapter, something to sing about. She was born in the early nineteenth century; a talented artist in her childhood, she was soon recognized in early adulthood for her psychic ability and her gift of healing.

Later, in her adulthood, people traveled for miles to consult with her on personal problems. But always health remained her primary concern. The knowledge she acquired gathering roots and herbs for her equally talented mother remained with her all her life—and, in a way, as testament to that knowledge, Bessie lived to the age of 105.

When I was in Tallinn, Estonia, a few years ago, a neighboring Baltic country to Latvia, I visited a large clinic. On the top floor of the building was a large art gallery.

Here patients in their bed clothes sat opposite works of art, meditating on them. Each patient was assigned to a particular painting that would best apply to the healing of that patient's illness.

Yes, music and art have healing power.

The Healing Power of the Mind

The mind can make you sick. And the mind can make you well. An American humorist said, "Nature heals and the doctor sends the bill."

When you are sick and not getting well, before going to a doctor to check your physical state of affairs, check your mental state of affairs. It may not be nature's fault that you are not well—it may be your fault.

Now don't start to feel guilty. The feeling of guilt itself—no matter for what—causes illness. It is one of a number of mental attitudes, all negative, that sap health. They include stress, of course, which is probably at the head of the list, followed by grief, fear, animosity, insecurity, loneliness, and so on. Yes, you cause your own illness, but there is no need to feel guilty because you are an innocent victim of humanity's ignorance of the power of the mind.

Other attitudes that cause disease or interfere with healing are discouragement, low self-esteem, and the suppression of feelings. Any difficulty of life can numb your desire to live. Many of these difficulties are not within an individual's ability to change, such as:

- Natural disasters and environmental disorders
- Strong local prejudices and acute racism
- Political upheavals, revolutions, and riots

Purposely not mentioned are economic upheavals involving runaway inflation or depression, and plague or contagion. Somebody always survives these and that somebody could be you.

The critical factor of whether or not you will be a survivor depends on your mind. It does not depend on your IQ or your education. It depends first on your desire, expectation, and belief; second, on your conscientiousness in relaxing and imaging in a positive manner.

Your mind can contribute to the solution of any local, national or worldwide problem, but it cannot bring about a solution alone. We mention this because it is worthwhile to make contributions to peace, harmony, and well-being of people everywhere. What you put out, you get back. This chapter will devote itself largely to your ability to use your mind to affect your body and even the bodies of other people any distance away.

What profits you to have life's problems solved if you do not have the good health and high energy to enjoy it? You can use your mind to energize sluggish organs, to accelerate the healing of an injury, to end health-sapping habits, to improve your complexion, to heighten your resistance to disease, to help your physician to be successful in healing you, to look and feel younger.

You already know the first step. Sit in a comfortable chair, close your eyes, and take three deep breaths. Now for the rest of the story.

The Mind/Body Connection

Earlier, we mentioned the work of Cleve Backster in monitoring the body's cells electronically, and how the cells react to the owner's thoughts even when removed from the body and placed miles away.

Right now, your cells know whether you are happy or sad, excited or bored, optimistic or pessimistic. Your thoughts and feelings supply the climate in which your cells grow, die, and new cells are created. A fair climate yields healthy cells and a healthy body. A less than fair climate of thought can cause every disease and disability in the physician's lexicon.

⌒Charlotte, 16, was worried about her father's survival after a heart attack. At any moment, the call might come in from the hospital bringing the bad news. Within days, she lost the hearing in both ears. Her father did not survive; but even after she recovered from the shock, Charlotte remained legally deaf.

Weeks later, her mother took her to a therapist who used deep relaxation and suggestion. While Charlotte was in this hypnotic state, she could hear the therapist ask her if she would like to hear again. She replied emphatically, "Yes!" He then told her that, at noon the next day, her hearing would return.

The next day, when the noon whistle blew at a nearby factory, she heard it.

The connection of the mind to the cells of the body has been explored intensely for the last two decades but cannot be found with a microscope. One day, it may be found with a telescope because, as Cleve Backster believes, it is a "primary perception" based not on chemical reactions or nerve energy but on the nature of the universe.

It is not a new discovery.

Over one hundred years ago, a Shakespearean actor in Australia named F. Matthias Alexander cured his own speech problem by mentally talking to his bones, saying, "Let my neck be free, let my head go forward and up, to let my back lengthen and widen." Since then hundreds of Alexander

Method teachers have helped people rid themselves of "incurable" health problems all over the world.

Since then hypnotism and self-hypnotism have spread the method even further with individuals such as Feldenkrais, Simonton, and Silva boosting and perfecting the mind/body connection. Moishe Feldenkrais contributed with his "Awareness Through Movement," combining mental and physical actions. Carl Simonton gave us all a quantum leap by effecting cancer remission in many "incurable" cases by having his patients relax and imagine their white blood cells winning the battle against the cancer cells. His method came to be known scientifically as "psychoneuroimmunology." Jose Silva's Silva Mind Control, now called the Silva Method, has trained millions of people in scores of countries to go to the relaxed alpha level and break unwanted habits, normalize malfunctioning body organs and systems, reach goals, and attain many of the miraculous mental capabilities listed at the beginning of this chapter.

Today, the term "psychoneuroimmunology" is being succeeded by the term "cyberphysiology" as the healing profession begins to acquire more experience with the mind/body connection and realizes that it is not limited to the immune system but that every cell, tissue, and organ in your body "hears" a mental request or instruction.

I have summed up this progress and provided instructions for cyberphysiology in my tape album *Mind/Body Communication—The Secrets of Total Wellness.*[1] Here are the basic steps.

You relax in the usual way. You mentally picture the part of the body that is causing a problem. You "talk" lovingly to the

---

1. Niles, Ill: Nightingale-Conant Corp., 1993.

part, asking it to correct itself, and mentally seeing it cooperating. The final mental picture is of the part completely normal and healthy.

Here are some "tips" to help attain success:

- Don't try it—do it; expect success
- Don't boss the cells; avoid an adversarial position— these cells are your friends
- Don't use memorized words; be natural, spontaneous, loving
- Do use a deep relaxation; additional countdowns are helpful
- Do use mental pictures; however you picture the part is fine, your mind knows "who" you mean

Your physician will probably know about cyberphysiology and might help you conduct it, but it's your mind and your body and you can use it as a preventive measure as well as a corrective measure. Cyberphysiology is not a substitute for medical care but an adjunct to it.

How to Get to Know Your Cells Better

Some of the ways that people have used the mind/body connection to improve their health include:

- Improve digestion
- Lower blood pressure

- Reduce cholesterol
- Inhibit pain
- Stop headaches
- Manage stress
- Lose weight
- Eliminate phobias
- Accelerate healing
- Stop smoking

Were I to supply the words to use mentally in each of these cases, I would be breaking the rule to be spontaneous. Using memorized words inhibits spontaneity. In fact, it obliterates it.

You do not have to be guided in how to talk lovingly to a friend. Your body and its parts are no different. In fact, they are among your best friends. However, there is a way to get what one might call a head start in mind/body communication. Why not visit your cells in advance and introduce yourself? We will call this a Fantastic Voyage, after the motion picture by that name that featured taking such a trip.

The new part of the procedure sounds complicated but it merely lists the parts of the body in a travelogue manner. Understand the logic to it and memorization is then unnecessary. Here goes:

Exercise to Know Your Cells

1. Sit in a comfortable chair, close your eyes, take three deep breaths and visualize your hair and how it goes into your scalp.

2. Imagine you are tiny and are sliding down a hair into the area below your scalp.

3. See a forest of hair roots below your scalp.

4. Thank your hair for being your crowning glory as well as protecting you from temperature extremes. Thank the skin of your scalp and have it pass on your thanks to all the body skin for a job well done.

5. Thank your skull for protecting your brain and have your skull pass on this thanks to all the bones in your body.

6. Move down and thank your brain for being such a fantastic computer.

7. Move down farther and thank your eyes, your ears, your nose, your taste buds, teeth, and tongue for the good work they do for you.

8. Thank your throat, then your stomach—a marvelous chemical laboratory able to digest whatever you eat— your small intestine and large intestine.

9. Thank your colon and kidneys and bladder for doing the thankless job of elimination.

10. Thank your reproductive organs.

11. Enter a blood vessel, riding along and thanking the veins and arteries and blood serum as well as the white cells.

continued

12. Disembark at your heart. Thank your heart for being a twenty-four-hour pumping station. Get back in a blood vessel and get out in a lung. Thank your beautiful lungs.

13. Get back in a blood vessel and ride to where you started, exiting below the scalp. Send a wave of love to all your cells.

14. Climb up a hair to above the scalp, open your eyes, wide awake.

If your itinerary is clear to you, put the book down and do it now. Or give the book to a family member or friend to read it slowly to you.

Using Water to Alter States of Consciousness

Sometimes one's life is not as joyous as it could be, not because we are not properly controlling our mind, but because somebody or something else is.

It all starts with our parents and teachers, but then goes on in less apparent ways all through our life. The bombardment of the media is a subtle form of control. Decisions about what you will wear, what you will eat, and where you will go are influenced strongly by them.

We are emphasizing health; here the invasion of your mind is massive. Your heart, you are warned, can have an attack. Fundraising for heart research fills newspapers, magazines, radio, and television. Every time you hear about heart disease, it strikes fear in you. You picture mentally what might happen. Subconsciously you are saying, "I may be next." And, to make sure you are affected in your giving, the media voices say, "It could happen to you." Now jump with me to the subject of water. In dreams, the subconscious is symbolized by water. We are also about eighty percent water. Water and the human mind and body have a close relationship. This relationship has produced a number of therapies and mental exercises involving water.

Immerse your body in warm water and you acquire feelings of security, joy, and serenity. It matters not whether you use a warm water spring, bathtub, or Jacuzzi, you are washed of tension, negativity, and, to a degree, the results of being bombarded by business reports, employee matters, or the media.

I was taught at MIT that water is the universal solvent, but the professor could not have meant the solution to problems. Yet the Silva Method uses a glass of water to do just that.

Flotation tanks are gaining recognition as a means of inducing an altered state of consciousness. Warm tubs are used in re-birthing, where you experience your birth again and identify any trauma that may have resulted in your exiting the womb.

There is an increasing popularity in waterbirthing. According to a report in *Brain/Mind*,[2] 1,100 obstetricians met in London in April 1995 and reported 9,000 cases of babies being born underwater, considered the best non-narcotic method of reducing pain for women in labor. Water is similar to amniotic fluids of the womb, reducing the traumatic contrast for babies after birth. Newborn babies are natural swimmers and know not to breathe underwater.

---

2. P.O. Box 4211, Los Angeles, CA 90042, Jan.-Feb. 1996.

Why not use warm water to wash away the blocks that still exist to your having the fullest success and joy in life? You can wash away subtle self-inflicted blocks or blocks inflicted by outside influences. Water is the universal solvent.

Improving Women's Self-Esteem

Life can be more trying for women than for men. It starts in an adolescent girl's education. Mathematics, science, and technology are considered male stuff and intimidating to the female sex. This builds a block to self-esteem.

Starting in school, there needs to be a better awareness on the part of a female student that these technical fields are now open to women and can provide lucrative careers. In the absence of this prior education, today's women may have to reprogram feelings of adequacy in these fields.

My gender is no drawback.
I have the ability to function intelligently
no matter how technical the work.
I am a successful woman
when I apply myself to such work.

It is not too late for women to upgrade their own can-do attitudes. Positive daydreaming has an immediate effect on being able to cope successfully with the male ego on the job, even with sexual harassment. To relax and imagine effective responses is to win out over male dominance.

The daydream begins to become reality. You, as a woman, begin to gain respect on the job that you have been deserving all along. Your body language, your facial expressions, your tone of voice begin to make a slap on your backside the last thing on an oppressive male's mind.

Even the glass ceiling can be removed for you. This is usually where successful women, climbing up the organizational ladder, can go no further.

> **There are no limits to my success.**
> **My gender works not against me, but for me.**
> **I am a valuable co-creator.**

As a mother, you can ease the way for your daughters by providing a flow of confidence-inspiring conversations and an awareness of body language.

Take a peek inside a warehouse. There's a woman talking to her male supervisor. Her whole body seems agitated and involved in what she is saying. Is she trying to "butter" him up, or throwing a smoke screen around her own frigidity? It matters not. To the alter male, she is admitting to an inferior place on the company's pecking order.

Later, another woman is talking to the same supervisor. She stands at a "safe" distance. Her body is erect and still. She uses her hands only to make a point. When he replies, she is listening intently but she shows respectful interest in what he is saying. This woman is in control; she leaves him with a definite impression of her importance.

Maybe that's not what you want as an unmarried woman. You are at the party to meet an eligible man. You stand really close. You have one hand on his arm. Whoever looks closely will spot an imperceptible stroking motion. In effect, you're saying, "I'm yours." Too bad for him, if he's not listening.

In order for women to strike a good balance between their femininity and their creativity, a daily affirmation will reinforce this desire and begin to manifest it more strongly in their daily life:

**I have a genuine feeling of togetherness with men and women. I respect them for any differences.
I see all people in the family of humankind.**

The Journey to Success Begins with a Single Thought

As the heightened assurance of men and women begins to take effect in their lives, there are pitfalls attempting to swallow them and return them to the abyss of want and suffering from which they are emerging.

If an old fear about insecurity arises in you, be it related to love, health, or money, you need to take immediate action to nip it in the bud. How do you neutralize fear? With affirmations of fearlessness. The deeper you are relaxed, the more effective are these affirmations. Here is a typical affirmation to improve your business if it is not responding totally to your work in Chapter 6:

**As I change my mind, I change my business.
Being wealthy is a function of enlightenment;
I am enlightened and becoming more and more enlightened every day. I am relaxed and confident about money.**

Other matters fit into this identical affirmation. The word "business" in the first sentence can be changed to "ability to love and be loved," and you would then change "wealthy" in the second sentence to "loving," and "money" in the last sentence to "love."

Or, substitute "circumstances" for "business" and follow with "joyous" for "wealthy" and "life's circumstances" for "money."

These affirmations can be used even as things improve in your life. They are the milestones in your journey that begins with a single positive thought and is reinforced along the way.

⁓Dorothy changed her mind and changed her fortune. After one successful year in business, she had just written a check for her home mortgage when she realized she would not have any more money coming in for seven weeks.

She felt panic. It was a common feeling for her, but hadn't been for months. She had money in a savings account that she was going to use for home improvements. Should she skip the home improvements and use those funds instead for business bills that would be coming due?

She sat in a comfortable chair, closed her eyes, took three deep breaths, and asked for an answer to that question. She waited. Soon she felt a sense of reassurance. It was as if an inner voice was saying that it was okay to make the changes in her house, and that money would arrive to take care of business bills.

Before two months passed, the business money was arriving, the bills were paid, and she had a modernized kitchen to better enjoy her living.

You, too, have an inner voice. It is the voice of a very close friend—your higher self. When you need an answer, do what

Dorothy did. Ideas will come to solve any problem you pose. They will feel like *your* ideas. You are making them up.

It is you. There is no separation between you and your higher self.

How to Program for a Better Day Today and Every Day

Sometimes, as you lie in bed after retiring, you go over what tomorrow will be like. Perhaps there is an important meeting at which you would like to be productive. Perhaps you have a blind date that you would also like to be creatively planned. Perhaps there are important deadlines to meet, sales to make, or goals to meet. Is this a case of good-bye to hours of sleep?

It does not have to be, not if you understand the incredible power of your own mind. You can close your eyes, take three deep breaths, and visualize the critical event of tomorrow. Play a mental movie showing everything happening for the best, just as you wish it to be. Don't end the session by opening your eyes and saying, "Wide awake." Instead, end your session by saying, "So be it," and go to sleep.

If you are comfortable with this procedure, why not use it to program every night for a perfect following day? Again, you close your eyes after retiring and take three deep breaths. Play a motion picture of tomorrow. There should be a clock in the picture showing the time hour by hour, starting when you get up, perhaps 7:00 A.M., and a calendar showing tomorrow's date.

Your first scene should be everything going smoothly with your family at breakfast—a harmonious start to the day. Mentally turn the clock to 8:00 A.M.—you are leaving for work at the proper time. "See" smiles on your family's faces; they, too, are right on schedule.

The clock now says 9:00 A.M. You are at your desk or wherever your work begins. "See" your staff or colleagues bustling about full of enthusiasm and energy. You know it will be a productive day. The clock says 10:00 A.M. You have had a good morning meeting (or whatever comes first in your business day). At 11:00 A.M. everybody is working harmoniously together. At 12:00 noon, your new customer arrives and the two of you leave for lunch (substitute the critical action for the day, if there is one, at whatever time it occurs).

Lunch has proceeded with good service, delicious food, and a successful meeting. At 1:00 P.M. on your mental clock, you are back at your desk, off and running. At 2:00 P.M., you and your colleagues are outdoing your usual selves in your productive work. At 3:00 P.M. more of the same. At 4:00 P.M.—well, continue with the movie of the day as you want it to happen.

Your mental movie is a shadow of things to come, because our thoughts create our life. Do you need instructions to program for a great week, a great month, a great year, a great decade, or a great lifetime?

Can Science Explain the Creative Power of Your Consciousness?

If you were to attend a conference on consciousness, you would want your money back. You would not hear about research into the extraordinary abilities listed earlier in this chapter. Instead, you would be subjected to endless lectures by specialists with impressive backgrounds on such subjects as neural correlates of consciousness, the role of extrastriate visual cortical areas, quantum theory, states and stages of consciousness, and the purpose of the primary visual cortex.

Got it? Don't throw your hands up. There is hope.

Despite the fact that they are sticking out their collective necks and may lose their grants and professional status, a number of philosophical scientists are daring to examine consciousness from the viewpoint of its phenomenology.

By far ahead of others in my opinion is Willis Harmon, Ph.D., president at this writing of the Institute of Noetic Sciences, founded by astronaut Edgar Mitchell on his return from the moon. I, who have been published for over fifty years, was also "out front" for many years and can vouch for the fact it is a lonely place to be. Apparently Harmon felt the same way when he attended a two-week conference on moral, ethical, and spiritual issues related to consciousness. He writes, "I was totally upended when, at the final meeting, as I opened my mouth to explain what I thought I had learned, I broke into uncontrollable sobbing!"[3]

Basically, this was at least partly due to the fact that the discussion leader, a scholarly professor of business and law, thoroughly believed in the same psychic phenomena as Harmon, which reputable scientists had debunked. It's like exploring in the vast reaches of the Arctic and bumping into your neighbor.

There will be frequent conferences on consciousness in the years ahead. They will be attended by experts in computer sci-

---

3. *Higher Creativity.* Los Angeles, Calif: Jeremy P. Tarcher, Inc., 1984.

ence, ethnology, cognitive science, psychology, neuroscience, medicine, physiology, biochemistry, and more. But don't hold your breath. They are on dead-end streets and blind alleys. It is doubtful that anything meaningful and applicable to you will surface for decades.

Look instead to the real researchers of consciousness in the world today: You and others who are learning to use their minds to change their lives for the better.

A Final Word on Cyberphysiology as a Path to Total Wellness

In 1988 some 100 scientists convened on the Hawaiian island of Molokai at the invitation of Earl Bakken, inventor of the heart pacemaker, to share their research in the effects that the mind has on the body.

So convincing was the overall result that the scientists voted unanimously to adopt the word "cyberphysiology" as an umbrella term for the still-not-thoroughly-understood phenomenon.

Scientists do not thoroughly understand electricity but we have been using it successfully. There is no reason why we have to wait to use cyberphysiology.

I close this chapter by giving you a better look at how to apply this mind/body communication to maintain a state of total wellness. I did not supply any specific mental image or body instruction early in this chapter because I did not want to encourage you to adopt my words. The element of spontaneity is essential.

As you mouth memorized words, something is missing. It would be like memorizing a romantic passage to say to a loved one. It would be too mechanical and lacking in feeling.

Understanding that the words used in the following instructions are not required or recommended, here is an example of how to apply cyberphysiology to a broken leg, in order to help your physician and accelerate healing.

Exercise to Apply Cyberphysiology in Healing

1. Relax where you are by closing your eyes and taking three deep breaths.

2. Imagine you are inside your body, looking at the bone fracture in your leg.

3. Mentally say, "My precious leg, forgive me for causing you this injury. Accept my love and restore yourself to normal use again."

4. Mentally "see" the bone fracture becoming less apparent, as if healing was taking place in a rapid manner.

5. Mentally say, "Thank you for healing well."

6. Mentally leave your body's interior and open your eyes, wide awake.

This not only works in any part of your body, whether tissue, bone, or organ, but—hold on to your chair—you can make it heal other people at a distance too.

Relaxation needs to be deeper and visualization needs to be as if it were real. This places us in a position of togetherness thanks to what Jung calls the collective unconscious, Sheldrake calls the morphogenetic field, Peter Russell calls the global brain, and Jose Silva calls higher intelligence.

Recently, a survey by doctors found that prayer increases successful healing by thirty-five percent. Maybe this is prayer. Whatever we decide to call it, it works.

～

9

Acquiring an Invisible Means of Support

⌒from Swami Amara of India

"Y ou are not the body." "You are not the body." "You are not the body."

I have been interested in Eastern thought for decades and not once have I attended a lecture by a Hindu without hearing those words.

If we are really not our body, then what are we?

Our life is devoted to keeping our body fed, keeping it warm, keeping it sheltered, keeping it sexually satisfied, and keeping it attractive. Why such attention to our body if it is not really us?

I wrote many books on home improvement before I began to write books on body improvement. Then came books on mind improvement followed at present by books on spiritual improvement.

From home to body was a natural step. The body is a home. It is not you, it is your home. Whatever you really are is at home in your body.

When we talk about mind and spirit, we are then homing in on who or what we really are. We are non-material. Being mind and spirit, there are few words available to discuss such a vital subject as who we are.

To discuss our life in terms of love, money, security, health, and circumstances, we are discussing the foundations of our home—the body. These foundations are our visible means of support.

These are essential. But perhaps even more essential are the foundations for who we really are. For those foundations, only an invisible means of support is possible.

West versus East— Material versus Spiritual

Earth is a giant compass with two magnetic poles. There also appears to be a type of polarity between the Eastern and Western hemispheres of this planet. This polarity is similar to the differences in the left and right human brain hemispheres, one being materially oriented and the other oriented to non-material matters such as feelings, ideas, intuition, and creativity.

The United States has taken the lead in the Western Hemisphere, developing civilization to its material apex. India has taken the lead in the Eastern Hemisphere, developing their knowledge and connection to the spiritual realm to such an extent that the left brainers call their masters "mystics."

Swami Amara, helping with this chapter, was such a mystic. Swami is a Hindu title of respect; Amara means deathless. Swamis are steeped in occult rites and practices that inspire mystery and wonder in the more materialistic Western mind. But this is not necessarily true for your mind, because you have been training yourself to use your right brain hemisphere and to become more attuned to the creative realm.

Swami Amara was a disciple of the great sage Rama Krishna in the late nineteenth century. Swami himself became famous for his ability to survive being buried alive for days at a time. He certainly knew how to tap an invisible means of support!

Complete the rest of the training in this chapter and you may deserve the title of swami yourself.

Which Came First, the Spiritual or Material Realms?

Which would you rather be in control of—the cause or the effect? When you stop and think about it, having control of the effect is rather limited. For instance, if the effect is snow, being in control of the snow means you can make a snowman, throw snowballs, or shovel. But, if you were in control of the cause of the snow, you could decide whether it should snow or not, where the snow should go, whether it should be wet snow or dry snow, and how deep the snow should be. The effect in the universe is the material realm. The cause lies in the non-material or spiritual realm.

Let's take a poll of some of our own past great men.

"Great men are they who see that the spiritual is stronger than any material force." Ralph Waldo Emerson.

"One truth stands firm. All that happens in world history rests on something spiritual." Albert Schweitzer.

"It must be of the spirit if we are to save the flesh." Douglas MacArthur.

Apparently they would all agree that, although a visible means of support is good, an invisible means of support can be even better.

Am I now going to provide you with a mystic formula to acquire infinite spiritual support? The answer is a resounding "no" and we will let a great Eastern philosopher, J. Krishnamurti, once head of a special theosophical society, tell you why.

> I was once the head of a world-wide organization
> founded in 1911 with thousands of members in
> many countries. It was dissolved by me in 1929.
> I said then that there was no path to truth and that
> no organization or organized belief as religion can
> lead man to truth or his salvation. I said then that in
> all so-called spiritual matters there is no authority,
> no leader or guru, and that all following perverts
> the follower. You have to be your own teacher and
> your own disciple.[1]

However, I am going to point you in the right direction: Within.

Where the Spiritual Cause of the Material Effect Lies

I was invited to India to teach meditation. India is the place where meditation began. However, I was invited to teach dy-

---

1. From *The Quest,* theosophical society periodical, spring 1989.

namic meditation, not passive meditation, which has been done in India for millennia.

After taking three deep breaths, you use your capacity to visualize and image to "see" what you want to happen. You are using your creative power to make things happen. This is called dynamic meditation.

In India, meditation may go a lot deeper than you may get, but the meditator just stays there and does nothing actively with the mind while in that state. This is called passive meditation.

Yoga began in India at least 5,000 years ago. It is quite common for yogis to get to the theta level of brain wave frequency—four to seven pulsations per second. In this way, they slow their metabolism and can be buried alive for a month with very little access to air.

Despite this passive meditation, India is still a place of great poverty and suffering. That's because passive meditation does nothing to correct this. When I taught a different kind of meditation in the Blavatsky Bungalow, at the world headquarters of the Theosophical Society in Adyar, the classes grew larger as the word got out that meditation has an additional benefit, once you know how to use it.

A story is told of how the Creator wanted to leave Divinity in a safe place on Earth. The Creator knew that hidden on the highest mountain, it would be discovered, and that hidden in the deepest sea, it would also be easily found. So Divinity was hidden in the last place a person would look—within him- or herself. Men and women alike can, by going within, and taking the right steps, assure for themselves continuing help from the other side—an ongoing invisible means of support.

The Right Steps May Not Be the Same for Everybody

I was lecturing in a foreign country to an audience that understood English. In order to build expectation and belief in the powers of the mind that would be demonstrated later in the day, I was elaborating on the latest scientific research that helped explain these powers.

Suddenly, the sponsors of the seminar announced there would be an unscheduled ten-minute break. They came over to me, quite agitated.

"Don't give theory," they insisted. "Demonstrate." They kept repeating this to me with great emphasis, indicating that they knew their audience and that if I gave only theory, there would be a flood of requests for refunds. No amount of assurance seemed to convince them that the path my lecture was taking was one that was proven to be most effective for all. They even followed me into the men's room to convince me to change.

So, I honored my hosts and changed. That day, fewer people saw auras, fewer were successful at doing psychometry (holding an object and telling things about the owner), and fewer people were able to receive a word that I was mentally sending. All of these abilities are in the kindergarten class of the powers of the mind, yet they require a basic understanding of how they work in order for them to indeed work. You need to understand the nature of the creative realm in order to evoke its cooperation.

As a child, I was amazed at how the servant always appeared at the right time to clear the dishes and serve the next dinner course. One day, as I was playing hide and seek with my sister, I crawled under the dining room table. There I saw a bump under the rug near where my mother was always seated. I pushed on the bump. The servant looked in from the kitchen and called, "Who's pushing that bell?"

There is no single bell to which the Creator responds. But there are a number of bells that are worth trying. One may work for you, or all may work for you. Here are a few tips. Maybe they'll ring a bell.

How to Speak the Creator's Language

In the first chapter, you were asked to begin to help other people in order to help yourself. This is not theory. It is fact. It is fact because we are all part of the same team called the human race. If you want to look at people as a speed race, there will be no winners. It will be a tie. We will all finish the race together.

Pushing the other fellow ahead does not leave you behind. The Creator sees to that. You are pushed ahead even more.

The Creator's language is creation. Every time you solve a problem—your own problem or somebody else's problem—you are helping the Creator. You are taking sides with the Creator.

It follows that every time you create a problem or become a contributor to a problem, you are working against the Creator. You are moving away from the Creator.

The more you talk the Creator's language, the better your life becomes. It works even better than prayer.

I am not saying you should stop praying. But you better stop and think before you begin to pray for something to be done. It is possible that, at that very moment, the Creator is praying to you to do what you were created to do, to get cracking and find a way to get it done by yourself.

Many people resort to such powerful tools as prayer in seeking to better their life. Often they make the mistake of asking that it be done for them rather than asking how they can improve their lives themselves.

One popular school recommends that you associate with successful people and imitate their mannerisms. When asked why he was constantly wiping his brow, one acquaintance explained he had studied a millionaire neighbor's mannerisms and his wiping the brow was going on constantly. Perhaps this was a secondary reaction to hard work. The only time success comes before work is in the dictionary.

One middle-aged female executive was known for smoking a cigar. The quarterly magazine *Cigar Aficionado* recently had an article recommending that a woman who wants to be taken seriously by male colleagues might pull out a fine cigar and light up. It said that men are disarmed and charmed by a cigar-smoking woman. We don't think the Creator is impressed. That's not the Creator's language.

The Creator's language is more action than words, but you might have to use words to encourage yourself to that action.

There are a number of negative mental attitudes about creativity that words can help dissolve. You might not think what you are doing is creative.

⁓Alice was a waitress. She had a desire to serve the
Creator, but here she was serving people instead.
She volunteered for church work in her spare time.
The church put her to work serving coffee at
meetings and meals to the poor on holidays. She
began to realize that even the serving of food in
the restaurant had a spiritual aspect. She enjoyed
her work more and her tips increased.

Other attitudes that inhibit your creative actions are the belief that you are not creative enough, or that what you are creating has no value. There could be other ramifications of this
same lacking-in-creativity concept, but they all respond to the
same corrective words. Here is an affirmation that re-asserts
your true value to the Creator:

**I know how to create because I am endowed with creativity.
I create what is needed and what I create has universal value.**

If you feel this is useful to you, repeat it daily three times at
the relaxed level for a week or so. You may feel that by doing
this, you become more aware each day of the Creator's presence. This could herald the greatest possible change for the
better in your life.

The Whole Is Greater than
the Sum of Its Parts

People have been inclined to go their separate ways. Motivated
by the material forces, the quest for riches and power has led
men and women to trample over each other, as well as over the
Earth's resources. This has led to the destruction of natural

ecological systems and violence to be environment. It has bolstered bias and led to alienation, factionalism, and wars.

Somehow this seems to be changing. It could be just in time.

An enthusiasm for recycling of materials and preservation of species is evidence of a new respect for Mother Earth. This indicates a movement toward togetherness and an understanding of the oneness of all life. Then there is a new appreciation for alternative methods of healing, especially where there is an appreciation of the whole person—body, mind, and spirit. The healing profession is beginning to see us not as separate body parts but rather with the more holistic view that we are not a collection of larynx, lymph, and liver but of body, mind, and spirit.

We are coming together. And the whole is greater than the sum of the parts.

You will be more and more aware of this unity with every passing day as your consciousness grows and you become more attuned to the source of creation. This awareness will loft you into a new and more fulfilling life with parameters of joy, wealth, and love far beyond where they are now, placing you in an arena of personal possibilities that may take your breath away.

This is so, because the whole is indeed greater than the sum of its parts. The parts have a consciousness of their own limitations. The whole has a consciousness of the Creator's presence and the limitlessness that it guarantees.

Put your two fingers together right this minute. Close your eyes, take three deep breaths, and ask yourself, "What is the direction of my greatest love?" If the answer that came to you was the Chase National Bank, good-bye and good luck.

The True Meaning of Greatness

A great football hero is later accused of a double murder.

A great community leader is later accused of absconding with charity funds.

A great religious leader is later accused of sexually abusing a child.

What is greatness as we understand it? Obviously, it is an ephemeral quality, here today and gone tomorrow. True greatness must have permanence and not be an illusion.

Jesus has said that there is nobody special, that we are all sons of God, so why strive for greatness? Good question.

The answer, reflected in the mirror of life, is that we should not strive for greatness—greatness, that is, in the popular sense, such as being a hero.

There is another sense: Greatness in the Creator's eyes rather than in the eyes of the created.

Here are some facets to greatness that do not necessarily evoke hero-worship but which are very likely to make points for you on the other side.

It comes not as news to you that helping others is a sure stepping-stone to greatness. Again, this is not limited to helping an old lady out of an elevator. It goes a giant step beyond getting involved with raising money for a meaningful charity or extending your working hours to volunteer at a care center. It involves becoming a helping hand to the Creator.

Stand up for what is right. This can be an unpopular activity if it deprives some of privileges while it frees others of imposition. One of the most successful movements of the last century in the direction of labor-management harmony was called Moral Rearmament. It espoused the concept of not who is right but what is right. Not only can this often be unpopular, but it can take courage. Whistle blowers are often discharged by the people who are guilty of the misdoings. This is eventually corrected as the truth becomes known and the Creator intervenes.

"Build a better mousetrap" points to another facet of greatness that not only produces a better pathway to your door, but better rewards. Don't save your skills; use them profusely. Become better and better. Skills are a gift of the Creator, who doesn't like to see them go to waste.

A spiritual "hero" is somebody who says "yes" to life. A person who says "no" to life might be the one who seldom leaves their house or apartment, as an extreme example. They have no confidence in the Creator to safeguard the created.

The person, on the other hand, who says "yes" to life, does not do wild and reckless things but is willing to experience new things; try the different and the challenging; meet new people; see new places; try out a new hobby, language, or sport. That person must be pleasing the Creator by taking fuller advantage of the greatest gift of all—life.

Reaching Your Goal Even When the Going Gets Tough

They say that when the going gets tough, the tough get going. Let them go.

You need not consider yourself tough. Tough means denser in material. As you have progressed along these pages daydreaming in a positive manner, helping others, becoming more and more attuned to the Creator, loving in a more "agape" or complete way, you are becoming less dense and more enlightened.

For you, when the going gets tough, just dial the spiritual 911. The spiritual 911 is not on your telephone dial but it is a sound. That sound is OM, pronounced "owm" with a long, drawn-out sound, like o-o-o-m-m-m. Why is it so powerful? If the cosmos could be heard—that is, if every molecule's vibration, every planet's circulation, every galaxy's rotation could be heard—that is what it would sound like to our ears, and the pronunciation of that word in a long, drawn-out chant is the closest we can come to imitating it.

Everything vibrates to that sound. Demonstrate this yourself by holding your hands out, palms down, while you or somebody else intones OM loudly. You will feel a tingling in your palms as they vibrate to its universal call.

The way to harness the power of this universal sound to enlist an invisible means of support is simple:

Exercise to Harness the Power of "Om"

1. Intone OM three times before beginning a relaxed problem-solving daydream session, when your eyes are closed, and three times at its conclusion, when you open your eyes.

continued

2. Reviewing your steps to solve a problem via daydreaming, there are usually three mental pictures.

3. Mentally see the unwanted condition. To indicate it
   is a problem, keep the picture dark or mentally mark
   a big black "X" on it, or both.

4. Mentally see yourself doing something to solve
   the problem or reach the goal. See yourself
   doing whatever comes to mind to do. If you are
   at a loss what to do, use the triggering technique
   explained below.

5. Mentally see the problem solved or the goal reached.

The triggering technique is used to accelerate the answer as
to what to do. You can program that the drinking of water, or
coffee, or beer, et cetera, whichever you are most likely to do
several times, will inspire you. As an example, mentally say,
"Every time I drink water, I am closer to knowing what to do."

The Wheel of Fortune and How to
Make It Spin for You

A state of consciousness is induced by the input of our senses.
Sights and sounds of limited money are the main sensory
input, but there are also the touch, taste, and smell of limited
money; the touch of worn-out carpeting, the taste of frankfurters and beans, the smell of musty wood.

Sight is by far the most important input. It is estimated that
some eighty percent of our total environment input is optical.
That is why imaging is so important.

Figure II: The Wheel of Fortune

Found in many cultures, the Wheel of Fortune is symbolically the wheel of life. Although you may find one in some art reference book, it is best to draw your own, knowing that you are creating avenues for the flow of wealth with each spoke you draw (see Figure II).

There is a sign for OM (see center of wheel, above). You are the hub of the wheel, the center of your universe. You can write the word "me." But the OM sign is a more powerful symbol to put at the center of your Wheel of Fortune. Label the spokes of the wheel with the qualities you aim for in your life, such as courage, honesty, generosity, compassion, strength, and so on.

Around the line you draw for the rim of the wheel, write your own affirmation of abundance. Here are some examples:

Spiritual affirmation:

**The Creator's power within me provides abundantly
for all of my needs.**

Scientific affirmation:

**The more energy I put out, the more I receive.
I grow in wealth of every kind.**

Philosophical affirmation:

**Abundance is nature's way. I am an expression
of nature. I express abundance.**

These should not be my affirmations. They should be your affirmations. Pick the kind you are most comfortable with. The spiritual kind is the most powerful. Next . . . .

Place the finished drawing of your Wheel of Fortune in some prominent place in your house so you see it frequently, even if only in a passing way. But before you do so, perform this metaphysical activation of it:

Exercise to Activate the Wheel of Fortune

1. Hold the sheet of paper with the Wheel of Fortune on it in your hand as you relax.

2. Place the Wheel of Fortune about six inches from your eyes while daydreaming.

3. See the spokes as extending outward into every aspect of your life, reaping a crop of abundance and wealth that surges through you as you go forth.

4. Open your eyes, wide awake, and post the Wheel of Fortune in a place you pass frequently.

This is now your Wheel of Fortune. You need not be conscious of it for it to work. If it is on the refrigerator door, every time you pass the refrigerator, you reinforce its power in you. The author has never heard of a case where the wheel of fortune did not work financial good in the life of its owner. Its effects may not be as dramatic as coming into a bundle of cash or inheriting an oil well. But everything becomes generally better for you as needs are met and financial limitations melt away.

Everyday Factors that Facilitate
Help from the Other Side

How we daydream invites specific help from the other side, but how we spend our wakeful time can also invite this help or hinder this help.

A person who eats red meat one or more times a day is becoming dense in the physical sense, compared to a person who eats lighter meats such as chicken and fish. A vegetarian can lead a spiritual life more readily and effectively than can a steak, roast beef, and pork chop lover. This has nothing to do with that meat eater's merits. It has to do with the meat eater's denser material existence.

If you are a habitual red meat eater and you are not bringing light into your life as dramatically as you would like, try emphasizing fresh fruits and vegetables in your diet. You need not make a sudden switch. Doing it gradually will probably pay off better for you, as it will result in a more permanent way of life rather than just a temporary trial.

Every time you go to sleep, you attain a more spiritual state. Higher intelligence can reach you in dreams and can elevate your consciousness and your health with little or none of the resistance offered by a busy daytime mind. One way to open yourself even further to higher intelligence while you sleep is to make sure that thoughts of serenity and comfort in the protection of the Creator prevail as you relax prior to sleep.

Daytime activity can be with negative pessimists or with positive, enthusiastic people. Help the former to become the latter. Your own positive enthusiasm is naturally contagious, but it can also be drained from you by constant contact with humans who act like leeches. Should you feel this happening to you, and it is impossible to extricate yourself from the business or social situation, surround yourself mentally in brilliant white light. It will help you to recharge.

Wherever the opportunity to choose exists, avoid associating with doom-and-gloom types and gravitate toward the creative and energetic. That's where the Creator is more likely to be making higher intelligence manifest.

It is not easy to provide ways to facilitate help from the other side in everyday activities. The basic meaning of everyday activities is material-oriented. I have started with these in the first chapter, but then have taken you step by step into a stage beyond the physical.

To use the word "metaphysical," meaning beyond the physical, may come close, but physics has taken such great strides in the past few years that what has been considered metaphysical a couple of decades ago is no longer beyond physics.

This means that "far out" is no longer as far out as it used to be.

The use of the mind to heal your body has an official medical term—psychocybernetics. Healing other people through mental imaging and prayer (assuming the two activities are different, which they may not be) is tolerated by the healing profession.

As I walk with you, hand in hand, to your great new life, I am daring to enter what has been comically referred to as "spaced out." The term is not a bad one, certainly not comical. It is far better to be spaced out than hemmed in. Hemmed in, you have a limited point of view. Spaced out, you have an unlimited point of view. Arguments can develop. Here is how to win them.

How to Win an Argument with a Materially Minded Person

There are five axioms to follow: Love, Understanding, Reason, Need, and Rapport. Let's look at each of these.

How do you love an adversary? How do you understand someone whose ideas are diametrically opposed to yours? How can you feel a closeness with somebody who might even be your enemy? And how in the world can you be equitable and just when your need is pressing? These are apparently contradictions—but not to the spiritually oriented person.

You have seen yourself operate on a plane of apparent contradictions doing the metaphysical work in previous chapters—contradicting the laws of physics regarding space and time and communications. You have actually risen above these laws by going into a mental level—a level where different laws operate, laws that might be quite opposite to physical laws.

Let us look at an example. You have experienced the pull of magnets. A magnet has two ends, or poles. If you place the north pole of one magnet near the south pole of another magnet, the two are attracted to each other and pulled together. On the other hand, if you put the north end of each magnet together, they repel each other. On the physical level, opposites attract. Likes repel.

What about laws on the mental level? Are you attracted by people who are different from you? People who look different, dress differently, talk differently, think differently? Of course not. You prefer to be with people you can relate to, and you are more likely to prefer a member of the opposite sex (physical level) with whom you have common interests and beliefs (mental level).

So you temporarily shelve this physical plane in order to activate the five rules for winning an argument on a more spiritual level—that is, convincing somebody miles away to see things your way.

You go to work on the mental plane, using these five

1. ***Love.*** Despite our physical differences, we are pe
   Despite our separateness, we are all parts of
   humanity: if one man pollutes, all men suffer; if one
   person is charitable, all people are elevated. See this
   common ground. Ignore the differences; dwell on
   the brotherhood. If you take a moment to do this
   right now, you will get a warm feeling within a
   few seconds.

2. ***Understanding.*** You are the way you are because of
   your upbringing, learning, and environmental input.
   He is the way he is because of his upbringing, his
   learning, and his environmental input—all different
   from yours. If you have a right to be the way you are,
   does not he have the right to be the way he is? Take
   a moment now to feel his right to be as he is, to
   understand him.

3. ***Reason.*** Reason is a two-way street. First, see the
   reasonability of the other person's stand. It is not
   yours, it is his. Now mentally review the reasonability
   of your stand. There are pros and cons in each stand.
   Review how the pros minus the cons for your
   position compare to the pros minus the cons for his
   position. Become reason-oriented to the problem.

4. *Need.* Think of your need in terms of how many problems could be solved if your need was met. How about secondary problems? When one problem is solved, usually others fade away, too. Involve as many people as you can in the chain of happiness that will result when your need is filled.

5. *Rapport.* Now permit all the positive feelings about this person to enter and to eclipse the feelings of hostility and antagonism. You are working together on this problem, on a higher level.

You are now ready to "move in" mentally (spiritually) and shift another person's feelings and attitudes in the direction you would like to see them move.

Read these instructions several times until you know the steps.

Exercise to Shift Another Person's Feelings

1. Relax with a photo of the person. If no photo is available, a mental picture is fine. Close your eyes and take three deep breaths.

2. Activate the five rules as provided above. Love the person. Understand the person. Contemplate his or her reasoning. Review your common needs. Feel a rapport with the person.

3. Ask the person to agree with you on the mental level now. Mentally speak not as a first sergeant but in a loving way.

4. Open your eyes while still at the relaxed level and look at the photo or see the person mentally agreeing with you. Again close your eyes.

5. Review your five feelings of love, understanding, reason, need, and rapport.

6. End your relaxation with eyes open, wide awake, knowing that the differences are dissolved.

Life becomes better for you as you help make it better for others. You automatically acquire an invisible means of support.

∼

10

Ways to Magnify
Your Magic

~summarized by Dr. Robert B. Stone

This chapter is going to hit you like a ton of bricks. I am pulling out all the stops and telling it like it is.

Aren't clichés wonderful? It's like they have a master key to your mind.

There had to be a sort of pussyfooting in order to take you gently into the non-material realm, calling it by that name, and calling it the spiritual realm on bolder moments.

If you have been daydreaming in accordance with the instructions to better your life, you have been introduced to this spiritual realm in a gentle way. But to help you enjoy the better life you fully deserve, I must now sock it to you.

For starters, say hello to God.

I have not used that word because of the resistance to it on the part of many people. Since God is the Creator, we have used Creator to get around that negativity. However, the Creator undoubtedly has no objection to being called God. I have no objection to the Creator being called God. Let's make it unanimous. By accepting God, you enhance your connection to the Creator. If one of your names—first or middle or last—was poison to people, would it not act as at least a partial separation between you and them?

God—Creator. Creator—God. We love our Father by whatever name, and for whatever time given us on this planet.

How to Make the Most of Your Time on This Planet

Humankind is not a permanent tenant on this planet. In fact, we just got here.

If you were to use a single year to represent the history of the Earth, then January 1 would be the day it was created and December 31 would be today. Let's look at some of the historical milestones along the way.

The first simple bacteria arrived some time in February and the first fish arrived late November. The first dinosaurs arrived about December 10 and by December 25, they were gone. The first recognizable human arrived December 31, and humans as we know them today came fifteen minutes ago, December 31, at 11:45 P.M.

So, don't think we have any priority rights. We are johnnie-come-latelies to this planetary hotel. We have to straighten up and fly right to merit a more permanent status.

Most of us are using only the left side of our brain to function on planet Earth. The Creator gave us a right side, too. Using only one side has caused a lot of problems. We have lived a material life to the exclusion of a spiritual life. Some of us make an exception for a few hours on Sunday, but what happens in a house of worship is usually left there.

Without spiritual guidance, those who choose to be without it are filling the battlefields, the drug cults, the prisons, the welfare roles, and the hospitals.

There are those who have activated their right brains and chose a more joyous and productive existence.

An example of such a person is you. As a result, you are making the most of your time on this planet. You are embarking on a fairy-tale existence, protected by guardian angels, assisted by unseen powers, and blessed by the Creator.

The Way Life Is on Earth

While daydreaming about the contents of this final chapter, these words came to me, from where or whom I know not. But I quickly wrote them down.

> We did not take God for granted. Every time a fire was lit, we thanked God with prayer and ritual. We did so when we arose in the morning and retired at night. We had no separation of the divine and nature. God was both Creator and friend. Man, nature, and God are one and interdependent.

Thank you, whoever you are. Timely and to the point.

Life on Earth might be a degree better if we still followed such rituals in recognition of the Creator and friend behind it all.

A Parliament of World Religions attended by some 8,000 delegates took place in Chicago in 1993. It lasted for a week, at the end of which time they identified the contributing factors to the present deplorable state of affairs in the world. These included:

- Unemployment suffered by hundreds of millions leading to poverty, hunger, and the destruction of the family
- Organized crime fueled by the abuse of drugs
- Tensions between generations, sexes, races, and religions
- Corruption in business and politics
- The suffering of the ecosystem now risking imminent collapse

It was agreed at this Parliament that a new global ethic was urgently needed. This would require the following changes in people:

- Every human being must be treated humanely
- Equal rights must be honored
- There needs to be a heightened commitment to a culture of tolerance and truthfulness
- A just economic order is essential
- For these improvements to happen, each individual must undergo a transformation of consciousness

This final need was issued with an emphasis that amounted to a clarion call, but not one word was spoken of how to raise one's consciousness.

The book you have in your hands speaks that word. It does so for you, not for your community, not for your country, not for the world. You begin to enjoy the fruits of a global ethic in your private world. As your example is caught by others, wider influence is manifested and ultimately the Parliament's vision could be attained.

How One Mind Can Help More than One Life

Why this body of thousands of spiritual leaders did not at least light the fuse to individual enlightenment and the individual elevation of consciousness is hard to fathom. Are our spiritual leaders too egocentric to understand that a person can exercise self-help successfully without them? Are they afraid they will be put out of business?

By now you know better than to think you can do nothing. You are probably hoping I will prod you into taking a step to make this a better world to live in right now.

You're right. Here is how:

A One-Minute Exercise to Better the World

1. Sit in a comfortable chair, close your eyes, take three deep breaths, and select some area of the world where there is an armed conflict going on.

continued

2. Imagine you are at a high elevation, overlooking the area. Imagine spreading a blanket of love like a luminescent mist over the whole area.

3. Mentally say, "Peace, peace, peace."

4. Open your eyes, wide awake.

This has taken you one minute. Yet it has cut the endurance time of that conflict by a lot more than that. Know that your energy of consciousness is connected to the energy of consciousness of other people, including the combatants', but most importantly to that of the Creator.

Furthermore, you are not alone in doing this.

Here are some other mental pictures to use:

- See an area of starving people, maybe in Africa. Imagine food being harvested. People are eating. Children are being fed. The granaries and storehouses are well stocked. Mentally say, "Health, health, health."

- See an area of crime, perhaps in a big city slum. It is dark and dangerous. Let the light in mentally. Imagine it enlightened and safe. Mentally repeat, "Love, love, love."

- See an area of poverty, perhaps in Russia or Mexico. See a shower of wealth descend. Use the picture of Benjamin Franklin on hundred dollar bills to symbolize nature's abundance. Mentally repeat, "Plenty, plenty, plenty."

I thank you for not just reading these ideas for helping humanity, but for using your consciousness to help manifest these solutions.

Where Consciousness Goes, A Real Energy Goes

Energy is creative. It creates what it is programmed to create. Your mind is the computer that programs your consciousness. The input data are your mental pictures.

A number of scientists met in Monte Carlo about twenty years ago to share their research in this ability of the mind to create at a distance. They decided to name this phenomenon and its study "psychotronics." I received the first doctorate in psychotronics awarded by a California university that was authorized by the state of California to grant degrees in consciousness.

Your psychotronic energy is related to your life energy. Without the latter, you would not have the former. You can feel your psychotronic energy, if you would like, with this simple demonstration.

Exercise to Feel Your Psychotronic Energy

1. Hold your left hand, palm facing right.

2. Point the fingers of your right hand at the palm of your left hand, keeping them six to twelve inches apart.

continued

3. Slowly move your right hand up and down as if fanning the air. But do it too slowly to cause air movement.

4. As you do this, you will fee a tingling feeling going up and down your left palm. It is caused by psychotronic energy.

Whenever demonstrating this to a seminar audience, there is usually a ninety percent affirmative response. Some people might have palms hardened and desensitized by years of physical work. I then have the audience hold their palms up to the stage as I move my fingers up and down.

"How many felt me?" Again, the question gets an overwhelmingly positive response. But that's kindergarten stuff. Now comes the clincher.

"I need a volunteer." When the volunteer arrives, he or she is asked to hold both hands up, palms facing me.

"I am not going to point my fingers at you the audience this time, only at the volunteer. But, audience, hold both palms up anyhow and see if you can feel anything."

I peer steadily at the volunteer and move my fingers up and down. Of course, I get a big smile and an emphatic nod of the head from the volunteer. Then I turn to the audience.

"Who felt my energy?" Perhaps 100 hands go up out of 300 present.

"How could you feel me? I was aiming my energy at this volunteer!" Deep silence.

"The answer is I was visualizing you. As I was moving my fingers I was mentally 'seeing' you, the audience. Energy goes where consciousness goes!"

As far as you, the reader, are concerned, your energy of consciousness should be devoted to creative purposes, but since expectation and belief are critical factors in such work being successful, here are a couple of fun uses:

Stand at the back of an elevator and, when a person enters and faces the elevator door, stare at the back of his or her neck. Be sure to simultaneously mentally picture what you are doing. In a few floors, that person will either scratch their neck or turn around.

Or, next time you are in a restaurant and need to summon your busy waiter or waitress, again stare at the back of their neck, visualizing as you do it.

When I am on the beach in Hawaii under my favorite palm tree, I enjoy watching the bikini-clad ladies go by. As I stare at their receding forms, they inevitably reach back and adjust their suits.

Several years ago, a national U.S. newspaper urged its readers to visualize a defect occurring in Big Ben, the huge London clock. On the very day and at the very time, the clock malfunctioned. Psychotronic energy is spiritual and therefore it is sacred. Let your uses of it be spiritual and sacred to you.

Reinforcing Your Connection to the Other Side

You have not been handed your connection to the Creator and the army of positive energies on the other side by me. You have always had it. You were born with it. You will have it when you leave this temporary residence we call Earth.

Still, there is nothing on Earth—certainly nothing in the Western world—that gives us a clue that we have such a connection or how to make use of it. We don't learn it in school; we don't hear it taught at the university level; we don't hear it in houses of worship. It is only hinted at.

So it behooves you to remind yourself constantly that you have an invisible means of support, that you are a unique human and loved by the Creator. With such daily reminders, you remember that you are the best and that you deserve the best; that divine money-making ideas come to you for the right brain asking, ideas that place you on the leading edge of life; that you trust in the infinite wisdom of the Creator with which nothing is impossible.

You can do this by considering this last paragraph as a daily reading exercise or a daily trigger for the ideas contained therein.

Or you can do this by using self-created affirmations daily, like the following:

Every time I close my eyes and take three deep breaths as I have just done, I go to a deeper level of relaxation faster. I get ideas. I solve problems. Higher intelligence assists my intelligence with answers and solutions. And this is so.

If you have programming to do that day, a good time to do it is right after making the above affirmation. After you have made the affirmation and completed your programming, it is effective to end with this:

I know my intelligence is a manifestation of higher intelligence. I believe in its creative power. I am making progress whether I see it or not. I expect positive results.

What these affirmations are really saying is, "I am not a creature of circumstance. I am a creator of circumstances."

It is also saying, "I let go and let God." You will find it hard to talk to anybody about the unbelievable grace of the Creator that manifests to you daily. "Coincidence" is the way many will shrug away a minor miracle. While you may be explaining how a coincidence is an act of the Creator to which he has not signed his name, the person will probably have changed the subject to politics, local gossip, or the weather.

There are no words to describe help from the other side. By talking to others about it, you dissipate your energy. You change what happened to fit the words. You accomplish nothing even though your missionary-like motives may be the best.

There are three requirements to continue a flow of assistance from the other side.

1. Use your mind to make this a better world to live in day by day.

2. Refrain from discussing the details of these private matters with anybody, even your family, but while still encouraging them to do the same.

3. Reaffirm your connection daily with prayer, affirmation, and love.

Time Is Different on the Other Side (If It Exists at All)

I received a phone call one morning from a distraught lady.

"I've been robbed of jewelry," she sobbed. "It has happened twice now. Five of my valuable rings and two gold necklaces were stolen from my bedroom. What can I do?"

"Have you reported this to the police?" I asked, hoping not to be called on to solve such a problem.

"It has happened twice. Each time the police took my report, but did nothing. I don't want it to happen a third time."

"When was the first time?" I asked.

"Exactly a week ago last night," she sobbed.

"Do you mind holding the wire? I'll be just a few minutes."

How long does it take to sit in a comfortable chair, close your eyes, take three deep breaths, and play a one-minute movie? Visualizing a calendar and seeing the date one week ago, then asking to see the crime being committed, I saw a figure in the semi-light of dusk crawling through the bedroom window. It was a young girl wearing a visor cap.

Back on the phone, I said, "It was a young girl wearing a visor cap."

"Oh, my God!" replied the lady. "It's my daughter!"

Later, the daughter confessed that she had been stealing the jewelry and giving it to her boyfriend.

This is a commonplace ability once you have trained your mind by activating your right brain hemisphere, as you have been doing. But don't attempt it yet. It takes practice, practice, practice. Then your mind can transcend both time and space.

The Creator and You— An Unbeatable Team

There are only twenty-six letters in the English alphabet. Yet they produced this entire book and a million others.

There are only ten digits, zero to nine. Yet these ten digits enable all calculations to be made, from arithmetic to calculus, and all statistics to be recorded since the beginning of recorded time.

There are only twelve notes in the musical scale. Yet every nursery rhyme can be sung with them and every symphony composed plus all the popular hit parade tunes in between.

What you can do with these twenty-six letters, ten digits, and twelve musical notes defies description. Is there any doubt that you and the Creator are an unbeatable team?

You have elected to be on the Creator's team by your work with this book. Hundreds of millions have not. They are on another team that has elected to play the game without the Creator. Let's take a look at the game they play.

Teenage sexual promiscuity and pregnancy rates boggle the mind. Dangerous drugs can be bought on more city streets than are free of them. Our heritage has been traded for quick fixes and instant gratification. We are spending money via government programs that are not only aggressive and invasive but have as many leaks into private pockets as a sieve, and are as ineffective as if they did not exist.

It wasn't always this way. "In God we trust" used to be the country's theme. With such trust, it was a different team. God was on it. Our founding fathers had an absolute faith in God and the team. Yankee ingenuity, fueled by higher intelligence, solved insolvable problems. Hard work, self-sacrifice, and personal integrity brought everybody the prizes they were seeking—freedom, health, prosperity. Then dreams came true.

Your dreams are coming true. Putting God on your team was a risk, but you took it. It's a win-win situation. Both God and you are the winners.

Benefits that Are Now
Attainable by You

If your goals are humane, you will reach them. There is no greater power in the universe that could be working for you. You stay on the same team with God by fanning the flames of oneness, feeling it more and more every day.

Look at what God can do. Rocks millennia ago were able to become cells, living creatures. Rocks that eventually became humans ultimately went to the moon.

If this can be done, your goals are a cinch. Good health? Done. Money in the bank? Done. Happy family? Done. Successful business? Done. Peace of mind? Done.

What about such things as winning an election, becoming a golf expert, typing with speed? Done. Done. Done. Your life is about to turn the corner.

I am constantly in awe of what God can do. I have seen an insurance man go from barely eking out a living to award-winning levels of financial success. A widow of fifty plus who had given up the idea of a loving companion is swept off her feet. A teenager goes from street smart to entrepreneur smart.

I myself would not be writing this book had I not gone from a teenager too shy and bumbling for words to an accomplished author and internationally recognized lecturer and counselor. These are not egotistical words of praise for myself, but rather humble words of praise for the captain of my team.

How Scientists Are Slowly Bending in God's Direction

Basic concepts, or paradigms, held by scientists for centuries are changing. Old Newtonian beliefs are going down the drain in favor of new Einsteinian beliefs. Let's look at a few of these changes.

Newton:	The world is matter and is made up of particles.
Einstein:	The world is made of energy fields that can crystallize as matter.
Newton:	The human mind is centered in the brain with its intelligence spreading to other parts of the body.
Einstein:	The human mind is part of a universal intelligence that fills the cosmos.
Newton:	Our bodies are separate.
Einstein:	Our body is part of a universal body.
Newton:	The laws of nature cannot be changed.
Einstein:	The human mind can transform the laws of nature because humans are its co-creators.
Newton:	We are human beings trying to be spiritual.
Einstein:	We are spiritual beings trying to be human.

We applaud this progress by scientists. Eventually they will get there. But we are not going to stand by and wait for them.

You Have Made a Quantum Leap
Ahead of Scientists

You have liberated your mind from the prison of the material world. You have re-connected yourself to your Creator after years of separation. It was you who moved away in the first place; now you have moved back. You have enlisted the help of the Creator directly or through angels, fairies, elves, or other people.

Because your consciousness has been liberated, expect genius-like insights.

The term "genius" derives from genie. A genie, like angels and fairies, works for the Creator. The genie manifests what the Creator mandates. These could be everyday events, such as bringing you together with the right person, or a miraculous favor, like making you the winner of a sweepstakes or lottery. You are a genius.

And what you will have experienced is a scientific event, just as sure as water can freeze into ice and ice can melt back into water.

All you have to do is behave like a genius and the world is yours. How does a genius behave? He or she acknowledges a problem, sizes it up, meditates on it, and acts on the insight received.

Meditation is now a familiar activity to you. Remember, "Sit in a comfortable chair, close your eyes, take three deep breaths, and visualize . . . ." By now you should have done this chapter by chapter some fifty times.

It is now one of the secrets to your charmed life. It is better than dialing 911. It is better than having a foot pedal under the table to summon a servant. It is better than having a relative who works in a bank.

Closing your eyes, taking three deep breaths, and visualizing positively produces genius-like insights.

Perhaps you'll say to yourself, "Wow. Look at what I thought of!" Go ahead. The Creator does not have an ego and so does not mind you taking credit for what the Creator presented to you.

Sometimes a solution involves other people and time. If so, that idea or genius-like insight won't be there when you meditate. Don't make the mistake of thinking that the Creator has failed you. Know that the wheels are turning.

Here is what you can do meanwhile:

Exercise to Work on the Solution to a Situation

1. Relax in a comfortable chair with a glass of water beside you, close your eyes, take three deep breaths and visualize the problem or unwanted condition.

2. Take a drink from the glass. A few sips will do. Put your two fingers together.

3. Mentally say, "Every time I drink water, the solution to this situation gets closer and closer."

4. Mentally see yourself drinking water and mentally see the problem corrected.

5. Open your eyes, wide awake.

The Unconscious Exposed for What It Really Is

As a genius, it behooves you to know more about your mind. You are quite familiar with the conscious mind. You are using it to read with, to move your body with, and to visualize with. But how about all of the activities of your mind that you are not conscious of: running your body, nightdreaming, creating solutions?

These other activities are usually associated with the unconscious mind. But that is an umbrella term. Actually, the unconscious is two separate areas—the subconscious and the superconscious. The subconscious stores your memories and runs the so-called automatic functions of the body. The superconscious, sometimes called the supraconscious, is your higher self, your connection to a common intelligence shared by all people and filling all space.

The hand illustrates these three aspects to consciousness quite well. Look at your hand and imagine you are one of the fingers and I am another one of your fingers. The nail on the finger you have chosen to be you is separate. That nail is like the subconscious. It is yours alone. It is private and separate.

The main part of the finger is your conscious mind. It too is separate. Your thoughts are yours alone.

Your finger is connected to your hand, which is your superconscious. Hey, you are not separate there! You are connected with me and all others and, via your body, with an entire "body" of intelligence.

Whatever you call it, it is where your genius is located. It is where ideas come from. It is what you contact when you close your eyes and take three deep breaths.

Frederic W. H. Myers, a contemporary Cambridge scholar, saw the unconscious as we see the superconscious—a source of intuition, creativity, and inspiration, but also as a subconscious collection of dusty memories.

We are now getting it sorted out. And the more distinctly we sort it out, the clearer the image of the influence of the Creator emerges. As one's consciousness expands—and you might say heightens—one's awareness of a higher intelligence also heightens. One actually begins to feel the oneness of the universe.

The Oneness of the Universe Has You at Its Center

I am at the center of the universe. So are you. Wherever consciousness is active, that becomes the source of creation.

Every unit of consciousness that I have needed to create this manual has arrived in the nick of time. So it now will be with you.

As the originator of this final chapter, with no seer identifying him- or herself, I know that I have been helped all my life, as I am being helped now, by one Joshua ben Joseph whom we know as Jesus. His teachings have come to us through numerous channels. But what has not been taught to us from the pulpits of the world are his words, quoted in various parts of the New Testament and in various ways, adding up to:

> Go to the kingdom of heaven within.
> Function within God's righteousness.
> And all things will be done to you.

This means to me: Relax and visualize. See problems being solved and illnesses being healed. And all that you visualize will manifest. To me, Jesus stands on his own as the most remarkable luminary of all time.

Lo Fu, Konedda, and Panopoulos were there when the work was started. Then along came Takapoosha, Quajagan, and Huktutu. Daydreaming for unlimited love was reinforced by Iriana; and then Bessie and Swami Amara arrived for the last chapters. Jesus, as stated above, has been here throughout the whole process.

These units of consciousness were augmented by unseen powers who delivered into my hands at the right moment technical newsletters, pertinent newspaper articles, professional magazines, television and radio reports, and events in my own life.

In fact, at this very moment, when this book is about to wind down to its final page, I asked for a powerful conclusion that would lift and vault the reader to new heights of desire, expectation, and belief.

Just then, a letter arrived from a friend in London, England, who is a Unity writer. In it was this amazing passage.

Read it slowly, pausing after each sentence, and realizing that you are making statements of fact that ring loud and clear in the universal halls of eternity, helping you, helping humanity, and helping yours truly.

> **I value myself for being a growing,**
> **unfolding individual.**

> **I embrace myself for being worthy of**
> **life, love, joy, peace, and well-being.**

I honor myself for being created in the image
and likeness of the Creator.

I praise myself for being capable of learning,
of enjoying life here and now.

I recognize myself as being innately greater than any
disabling thought or feeling of inadequacy or fear.

I respect myself for being who I am in reality and for
endeavoring, step by step, to express that reality.

I love myself as the precious creation of a loving Creator.

I see myself as possessing qualities of patience,
compassion, tenderness, and beauty.

I make a commitment to myself by holding a vision of
myself as a precious and beloved child of the Creator.

Yes, I am a beloved child of the Creator.
I accept this reality now as I commit myself anew
to believing in myself.

Thank you, Father.

~

 **ibliography**

Historical

Eaton, Evelyn. *Go Ask the River.* Berkeley, Calif.: Celestial Arts, 1990.

Four Masterworks of American Indian Literature. New York: Ferrar Strauss & Giroux, 1974.

Rexroth, Kenneth. *One Hundred Poems from the Chinese.* New York: New Directions, 1971.

Shah, Idvis. *Special Illuminations: The Sufi Use of Humor.* London: Octagon Press, 1977.

———. *Nasrudin.* New York: E. P. Dutton & Co., 1972.

Yutan, Lin. *The Wisdom of China and India.* New York: Random House, 1942.

General

Benson, Herbert, M.D. Timeless Healing. *New York:* Scribners, 1996.

Boone, J. Allen. *Kinship with All Life.* New York: Harper & Row, 1954.

Harmon, Willis, Ph.D., and Howard Rheingold. *Higher Creativity.* Los Angeles, Calif.: Jeremy P. Tarcher Inc., 1984.

Nelson, John, ed. *Solstice Shift.* Charlottesville, Va.: Hampton Road Publishing, 1997.

Redfield, James. *The Tenth Insight.* New York: Time-Warner, 1997.

Sheldrake, Rupert. *A New Science of Life.* London: Muller, 1982.

Stone, Robert B., Ph.D. *The Secret Life of Your Cells.* Atglen, Penn.: Schiffer Publishing, 1989.

Audio Tape Albums

Loehr, Jim, Ed.D.; Nick Hall, Ph.D.; Jack Groppel, Ph.D. *Optimal Health.* Niles, Ill.: Nightingale-Conant, 1994.

Stone, Robert B., Ph.D. *Mind/Body Communication.* Niles, Ill.: Nightingale-Conant, 1993.

☾ REACH FOR THE MOON

Llewellyn publishes hundreds of books on your favorite subjects! To get these exciting books, including the ones on the following pages, check your local bookstore or order them directly from Llewellyn.

ORDER BY PHONE

- Call toll-free within the U.S. and Canada, 1-800-THE MOON
- In Minnesota, call (612) 291-1970
- We accept VISA, MasterCard, and American Express

ORDER BY MAIL

- Send the full price of your order (MN residents add 7% sales tax) in U.S. funds, plus postage & handling to:

  Llewellyn Worldwide
  P.O. Box 64383, Dept. K698-X
  St. Paul, MN 55164–0383, U.S.A.

POSTAGE & HANDLING
(For the U.S., Canada, and Mexico)

- $4.00 for orders $15.00 and under
- $5.00 for orders over $15.00
- No charge for orders over $100.00

We ship UPS in the continental United States. We ship standard mail to P.O. boxes. Orders shipped to Alaska, Hawaii, The Virgin Islands, and Puerto Rico are sent first-class mail. Orders shipped to Canada and Mexico are sent surface mail.

International orders: Airmail—add freight equal to price of each book to the total price of order, plus $5.00 for each non-book item (audio tapes, etc.).

Surface mail—Add $1.00 per item.

Allow 2 weeks for delivery on all orders.
Postage and handling rates subject to change.

DISCOUNTS

We offer a 20% discount to group leaders or agents. You must order a minimum of 5 copies of the same book to get our special quantity price.

FREE CATALOG

Get a free copy of our color catalog, *New Worlds of Mind and Spirit*. Subscribe for just $10.00 in the United States and Canada ($30.00 overseas, airmail). Many bookstores carry *New Worlds*—ask for it!

Visit our web site at www.llewellyn.com for more information.

Celestial 911
Call with Your Right Brain
for Answers!

Robert B. Stone, Ph.D.

Your mind possess staggering abilities that defy science. Yet most of us live without activating our right brain hemispheres, which is like living with one hand tied behind our backs. Your right brain is essential for healing, for creativity, problem solving and enjoying meaningful personal relationships. Most importantly, your right brain is your connection to the spiritual realm, to where you came from and to your guardian angels. *Celestial 911* will teach you how to turn on your right brain hemisphere and contact help from the other side.

A series of 32 "action plans" will help you to open your innate doorway to the invisible world of spirit helpers. Through the simple technique of Controlled Daydreaming, you can begin to manifest your true genius . . . turn up your sexual attraction . . . brighten your financial picture . . . and heal at a distance.

1-56718-697-1
240 pp., 5³⁄₁₆ x 8, softcover $7.95

The Lost Secrets of Prayer
Practices for Self-Awakening

Guy Finley

Do your prayers go unanswered? Or when they are answered, do the results bring you only temporary relief or happiness? If so, you may be surprised to learn that there are actually two kinds of prayer, and the kind that most of us practice is actually the least effective.

Bestselling author Guy Finley presents *The Lost Secrets of Prayer*, a guide to the second kind of prayer. The purpose of true prayer, as revealed in the powerful insights that make up this book, is not to appeal for what you think you want. Rather, it is to bring you to the point where you are no longer blocked from seeing that everything you need is already here. When you begin praying in this new way, you will discover a higher awareness of your present self. Use these age-old yet forgotten practices for self-awakening and your life will never be the same.

1-56718-276-3
240 pp., 5¼ x 8 $9.95

Designing Your Own Destiny
The Power to Shape Your Future

Guy Finley

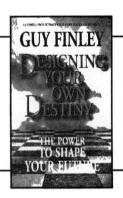

This book is for those who are ready for a book on self-transformation with principles that actually *work*. *Designing Your Own Destiny* is a practical, powerful guide that tells you, in plain language, exactly what you need to do to fundamentally change yourself and your life for the better, permanently.

Eleven powerful inner life exercises will show you how to master the strong and subtle forces that actually determine your life choices and your destiny. You'll discover why so many of your daily choices up to this point have been made by default, and how embracing the truth about yourself will banish your self-defeating behaviors forever. Everything you need for spiritual success is revealed in this book. Guy Finley reveals and removes many would-be roadblocks to your inner transformation, telling you how to dismiss fear, cancel self-wrecking resentment, stop secret self-sabotage and stop blaming others for the way you feel.

After reading *Designing Your Own Destiny,* you'll understand why you are perfectly equal to every task you set for yourself, and that you truly *can* change your life for the better!

1-56718-278-X
160 pp., mass market, softcover $6.99

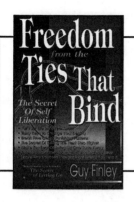

Freedom From the Ties that Bind
The Secret of Self Liberation

Guy Finley

Imagine how your life would flow without the weight of those weary inner voices constantly convincing you that "you can't," or complaining that someone else should be blamed for the way you feel. The weight of the world on your shoulders would be replaced by a bright, new sense of freedom. Fresh, new energies would flow. You could choose to live the way you want. In *Freedom from the Ties that Bind,* Guy Finley reveals hundreds of Celestial, but down-to-earth, secrets of Self-Liberation that show you exactly how to be fully independent, and free of any condition not to your liking. Even the most difficult people won't be able to turn your head or test your temper. Enjoy solid, meaningful relationships founded in conscious choice—not through self-defeating compromise. Learn the secrets of unlocking the door to your own Free Mind. Be empowered to break free of any self-punishing pattern, and make the discovery that who you really are is already everything you've ever wanted to be.

0-87542-217-9
240 pp., 6 x 9, softcover $10.00

The Intimate Enemy
Winning the War Within Yourself

Guy Finley and
Ellen Dickstein, Ph.D.

Within each of us lurk invisible psychological characters that inhabit our inner beings and make choices for us—choices that repeatedly cause us pain on some level. Now, best-selling self-help author Guy Finley and psychologist Dr. Ellen Dickstein expose these characters for what they really are: our mechanical, unconscious reactions and misperceptions that create a threatening world.

The Intimate Enemy will introduce you to astounding parts of yourself that you never knew existed. You will observe the inner dramas that control your life without your knowledge. Best of all, you will awaken to a higher awareness that provides the only true strength and confidence you need to walk into a fearless future. As you uncover the exciting truth about who you really are, you will gain an unshakable understanding of the human struggle and witness proof of a higher world, free from all strife.

1-56718-279-8
256 pp., 5³⁄₁₆ x 8 **$9.95**

Healing the Feminine
Reclaiming Woman's Voice

Lesley Irene Shore, Ph.D.
(formerly *Reclaiming Woman's Voice*)

Most self-help books for women inadvertently add to women's difficulties by offering ways to battle symptoms of distress without examining the underlying causes. One of the first of its kind, *Healing the Feminine* chronicles the struggles and triumphs of a psychologist and her clients on their personal journeys to self-discovery and wholeness.

Tracing much of women's distress to society's devaluation of the feminine, Dr. Shore illustrates the need for both men and women to reclaim their hidden but vital feminine aspects. Reconnecting with the feminine entails affirming the female experience, the female body, and the female way of being. Through a variety of methods that include breathing exercises, mental imagery, and living in tune with nature, we can learn to hear our hidden "Woman's Voice" and begin the journey to wholeness and peace.

1-56718-667-X
208 pp., 5¼ x 8, softcover   **$12.00**

Healing the Past
Getting on with Your Life

Arian Sarris

Is your life how you want it to be? Are you happy? Or are you ready to break free of those compulsions and urges that keep you locked into old ways of thinking, acting and believing?

Healing the Past gives you the tools to heal old emotional pain. Explore how your patterns, programs and fears were shaped by your childhood environment and how you can now release those old constraints. Plus, discover how working with past lives can resolve problems with which you continually struggle.

Learn how to speed up your healing by connecting with your most important partner: your higher self. Call on your guardian angels to help heal your karmic issues instantly. Raise your vibrational frequency to shift what you attract into your life. Put your "five selves" into alignment so you can manifest your life purpose. Create a "present time field" to release negative energy trapped around you.

1-56718-601-7
240 pp., 5¼ x 8, softcover   **$12.95**

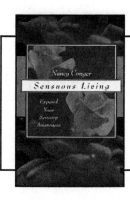

Sensuous Living
Expand Your Sensory Awareness

Nancy Conger

Take a wonderful journey into the most intense source of delight and pleasure humans can experience: the senses! Enjoying your sense of sight, sound, smell, taste and touch is your birthright. Learn to treasure it with this guide to sensuous living.

Most of us revel in our senses unabashedly as children, but societal norms gradually train us to be too busy or disconnected from ourselves to savor them fully. By intentionally practicing sensuous ways of living, you can regain the art of finding beauty and holiness in simple things. This book provides activities to help you engage fully in life through your senses. Relish the touch of sun-dried sheets on your skin. Tantalize your palate with unusual foods and taste your favorites with a new awareness. Attune to tiny auditory pleasures that surround you, from the click of computer keys to raindrops hitting a window. Appreciate light, shadow and color with an artist's eye.

Revel in the sensory symphony that surrounds you and live more fully. Practice the fun techniques in this book and heighten every moment of your life more—you're entitled!

1-56718-160-0
224 pp., 6x9, illus., softcover   **$12.95**

The Power of Dreaming
Messages from Your Inner Self

D. Jason Cooper

Unlock the secret of your dreams and open the door to your inner self! Our dreams hold a wisdom which can guide us, protect us and better our lives, if we listen to it. *The Power of Dreaming* presents a new, reliable, and effective "technology" for interpreting your dreams, as it is the first book to separate dream symbols from their context to better interpret each element: the nature of the dream and your role within it; its events, people and objects; archetypes in the dream; and the dream's class (whether it's a problem-solving dream, a house-cleaning dream, a psychological dream or an occult dream). Once you string meanings of all these elements together, you'll arrive at a complete, accurate and insightful interpretation of your dreams. This brand-new technique illustrates how events, rather than objects, are the key to unlocking your dreams' meanings. Includes three different dream dictionaries: one to interpret the meaning of events, one for objects, and one for archetypes.

1-56718-175-9
224 pp., 6 x 9, softcover $12.00

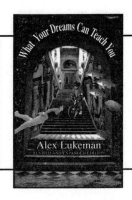

What Your Dreams Can Teach You

Alex Lukeman

Dreams are honest and do not lie. They have much to teach us, but the lessons are often difficult to understand. Confusion comes not from the dream but from the outer mind's attempt to understand it.

The new, expanded edition of *What Your Dreams Can Teach You* is a workbook of self-discovery, with a systematic and proven approach to the understanding of dreams. It does not contain lists of meanings for dream symbols. Only you, the dreamer, can discover what the images in your dreams mean for you. The book does contain step-by-step information that can lead you to success with your dreams, success that will bear fruit in your waking hours. Learn to tap into the aspect of yourself that truly knows how to interpret dreams, the inner energy of understanding called the "Dreamer Within." This aspect of your consciousness will lead you to an accurate understanding of your dreams and even assist you with interpreting dreams of others.

0-87542-475-9
336 pp., 6 x 9, softcover $14.95

Practical Guide to Creative Visualization
Proven Techniques to Shape Your Destiny

Denning & Phillips

All things you will ever want must have their start in your mind. The average person uses very little of the full creative power that is his, potentially. It's like the power locked in the atom—it's all there, but you have to learn to release it and apply it constructively.

If you can see it . . . in your Mind's Eye . . . you will have it! It's true: you can have whatever you want, but there are "laws" to mental creation that must be followed. The power of the mind is not limited to, nor limited by, the material world. Creative Visualization enables humans to reach beyond, into the invisible world of Astral and Spiritual Forces.

Through an easy series of step-by-step, progressive exercises, your mind is applied to bring desire into realization! Wealth, power, success, happiness even psychic powers . . . even what we call magical power and spiritual attainment . . . all can be yours. You can easily develop this completely natural power, and correctly apply it, for your immediate and practical benefit. Illustrated with unique, "puts-you-into-the-picture" visualization aids.

0-87542-183-0
294 pp., 5¼ x 8, illus., softcover $9.95

To order, call 1-800-THE MOON
Prices subject to change without notice

Spirit Guides & Angel Guardians
Contact Your Invisible Helpers

Richard Webster

They come to our aid when we least expect it, and they disappear as soon as their work is done. Invisible helpers are available to all of us; in fact, we all regularly receive messages from our guardian angels and spirit guides but usually fail to recognize them. This book will help you to realize when this occurs. And when you carry out the exercises provided, you will be able to communicate freely with both your guardian angels and spirit guides.

You will see your spiritual and personal growth take a huge leap forward as soon as you welcome your angels and guides into your life. This book contains numerous case studies that show how angels have touched the lives of others, just like yourself. Experience more fun, happiness and fulfillment than ever before. Other people will also notice the difference as you become calmer, more relaxed and more loving than ever before.

1-56718-795-1
368 pp., 5³⁄₁₆ x 8 $9.95

A Rich Man's Secret
A novel by

Ken Roberts

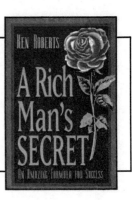

Victor Truman is a modern-day Everyman who spends his days scanning the want ads, hoping somehow to find his "right place." He has spent years reading self-help books, sitting through "get rich quick" seminars, living on unemployment checks, practicing meditation regimens, swallowing megavitamins, listening to talk radio psychologists . . . each new attempt at self-fulfillment leaving him more impoverished in spirit and wallet than he was before.

But one day, while he's retrieving an errant golf ball, Victor stumbles upon a forgotten woodland cemetery and a gravestone with the cryptic message, "Take the first step—no more, no less—and the next will be revealed." When Victor turns sleuth and discovers that this stone marks the grave of wealthy industrialist Clement Watt, whose aim was to help spiritual "orphans" find their "right place," he is compelled to follow a trail of clues that Mr. Watt seems to have left for him.

This saga crackles with the excitement of a detective story, inspires with its down-home wisdom and challenges the status quo through a penetrating look at the human comedy that Victor Truman—like all of us—is trying to understand.

1-56718-580-0
208 pp., 5¼ x 8, softcover $9.95